BUCKET

~ TO ~

GREECE

Volume 1

V.D. BUCKET

Editor: James Scraper
Cover: German Creative
Print Format: The Book Khaleesi

Chapter 1

Victor Is Persuaded to Pen a Book

Everyone is doing it," my brother-in-law, Barry, insisted. "You can't up-sticks and move to Greece without writing a book about it, Victor."

"I'm having nothing to do with it," my wife Marigold scoffed. "He'll turn us into a pair of laughing stocks."

"It will give him something to do and keep him from getting under your feet," Barry reasoned. "Victor needs a hobby now he's retired, otherwise he'll stick to you like a limpet, cramping your style."

Marigold's response to Barry's suggestion was somewhat surprising considering her compulsive addiction to 'moving abroad' books. The shelves she would no doubt nag me to build in our new Greek home would soon be groaning under the weight of tomes about starting a new life in such diverse destinations as Outer Mongolia, Mauriac, and Murcia, even though our eventual move transported us from Manchester to Messinia.

Barry continued to persuade me our move to Greece should be recorded for posterity.

"But I've never written a book before," I argued.

"You spent half your working life writing," Barry pointed out.

"I hardly think writing reports on the risk of contracting food poisoning from unhygienic restaurants and grubby takeaways is quite the same thing," I said, recalling my glittering career as a public health inspector.

"It took a lot of imagination to come up with so many original ways to describe filthy kitchens," Marigold conceded, whilst still voicing her doubts about the unwanted attention a book could attract.

"He must use a pen name to preserve his anonymity," Barry suggested. "Marigold, you could cast an eye over the book before he unleashes it on the reading public, to give it your seal of approval. No one need ever know what he's up to; after all Victor is far too modest and reserved to risk being mobbed by fans every time he sets foot outside."

Marigold snorted at the very notion, before considering the suggestion of a pen name. "Perhaps adopting a non de plume would keep us incognito if Victor's scribbling does achieve recognition," Marigold mused.

"Why not pull out the old Bucket name?" Barry proposed. "You have both ensured no one but the immediate family has a clue about the original existence of V.D. Bucket."

I must digress here to explain no one knows me by the name Victor or my wife by the name Marigold. Our mutual pact of silence hides our occasional blushes if the topic of buckets is ever raised.

The exceedingly unfortunate name of Victor Donald was pencilled on a piece of cardboard,

safety-pinned to the pink frilly bonnet tied securely to my head, on the night I was discovered abandoned in a bucket outside the railway station. A dark balaclava may have been more suitable attire, since no one had bothered to scrub the coal dust out of the bucket. It was conjectured I was dumped there by someone with a train to catch: possibly seeking a more glamorous life in a big city, without the encumbrance of a baby. Personally, I have always believed the pink bonnet was a vital clue, hinting parental abandonment due to the disappointment of my not being a girl. Whilst the fruitless search for the absconded parent was underway, some bright spark administrator added to the indignity by tagging me with the surname Bucket, inspired by the metal receptacle I'd been left in.

Fortunately my given name was as swiftly abandoned as I: the terrible connotations of having the first two initials of VD soon becoming apparent. The nurses who made a terrible fuss of me asked, "Who in their right mind saddles an innocent baby with the indelicate initials VD?" for that was in the days before sexually transmitted infections were invented and the

promiscuous were more inclined to catch vene-
real diseases. If I'd been saddled with Vic no
doubt the shame would be compounded with
an endless litany of chest rub jokes.

The details of my ignominious start in life
are something I prefer not to dwell on, though
naturally I felt obliged to share my shameful secret with my very proper wife before our nup-
tials. Much as she assures me she loves me, Marigold has always maintained that if I hadn't
been adopted and name changed there was no
way she would have lumbered herself with a
husband bearing the initials VD, or taken the
surname Bucket. "The only way I would have
come near you would have been in a pair of
Marigolds," she'd joked, landing herself with
the affectionate pet name of Marigold, in honour of the popular brand of yellow rubber
gloves.

"Barry, you could be onto something," I admitted. "I always found my inauspicious beginnings of being abandoned in a bucket most mor-
tifying. However a recent encounter with a self-
help guru persuaded me to embrace the nega-
tives and turn them into positives. I will ex-
punge the adverse associations of V.D. Bucket

and take it as my pseudonym for this experimental foray into the literary world."

Having settled the matter of penning an 'upsticks to Greece' book under an incognito pen name, we clambered up the rather hazardous stone steps leading to the roof terrace and settled into the rickety plastic chairs surreptitiously scavenged from the local bins. Naturally I checked Barry's chair wasn't placed anywhere near the edge, since he suffers terribly from vertigo. It simply wouldn't make a good first impression on the locals if Barry hurled on them over the wall.

The roof terrace proved the deciding factor when Marigold determined we would make our new home in a tiny village high in the mountains of Messinia, the village henceforth to be known by the covert name of Meli to protect our privacy. Marigold's decision took me by complete surprise. Before discovering the dated village house she had adamantly refused to settle for anything less than a brand new villa with a pool, by the sea. Instead she fell for a rambling old village house in the middle of nowhere, desperately in need of modernisation, with a very precarious water supply.

Chapter 2

The Lure of Greece

T he lure of Hellenic life lay at the very heart of Marigold's long-held dream of starting afresh in a new country, seducing her with visions of stunning sunsets and captivating vistas of unrivalled beauty. A fortnight's package in Patmos, Parga or Paros was never enough to satisfy her Grecian dreams, incidentally the first proposed title of these ramblings, until my brother-in-law Barry insisted it sounded too much like the date-expired bottle of Grecian 2000 he'd discovered lurking at the back of my bathroom cabinet.

The Grecian appeal will not be lost on anyone who has ever ventured to this ethereal landscape, a poetic paradise steeped in the history of Hellenic heroes. The all-embracing warmth of '*filoxenia*', Greek hospitality, consumed Marigold with wistful nostalgia each time our holidays ended, sending her tripping off to the travel agent in search of our next adventure. Colourful pins were planted in an enormous map of Greece and her islands that decorated the dining room wall, as Marigold fantasised about swapping our unassuming semi for a palatial villa in mythical lands. Needless to say I had little say in the matter: an irrelevant detail since the secret of our happy marriage lay in my indulging Marigold's whims, at least if I wished to continue enjoying a quiet life.

Around the turn of the millennium Marigold became more vocal about moving to Greece, inspired by the spew of 'A Place in the Sun' type television programmes, on top of her nightly addiction of bedtime reading about relocating to sunnier climes. Her eyes took on a calculating gleam when the prospect of an early retirement payoff from my illustrious career as a public health inspector was broached, particularly since Marigold had idle time on her hands following 'the incident' that resulted in her unexpected resignation from her position as a pet food taster.

Dithering over destinations delayed any concrete plans for departure until we discovered the Greek Mani. Marigold was immediately transfixed, besottedly declaring she had finally found the perfect place to live out the twilight years of our existence. Whilst setting up an appointment with a foreign estate agent, she cajoled me into accepting the offer of early retirement. Before I knew it a 'For Sale' sign was standing erect in the front garden and Marigold was busy flogging off my accumulated collection of vintage model trains on EBay, insisting we weren't going to cart all my toy trains to mainland Europe and have them cluttering up the marble floors of our new villa.

"But we haven't found a villa yet," I'd argued.

"Victor, it is only a matter of time, don't be so negative."

"Perhaps we should consider renting a place in Greece and keeping hold of our home here, in case things don't work out," I'd suggested, only to be shot down by a withering look. Marigold was determined this was a no-going back moment. Every doubt I voiced, from the difficulties of living in a country where we couldn't speak the language, to adjusting to the stifling heat of a Greek summer and my concerns about restaurant hygiene, was fobbed off with practical solutions about language classes, air-conditioning and indigestion tablets. I was not exactly averse to the idea of moving to Greece; I simply exercised a more cautious approach, one which Marigold merrily steamrolled over.

"And you needn't think that ticking monstrosity is taking pride of place above our new fireplace," Marigold said scathingly when I arrived home from my leaving-do clutching the obligatory clunky fake gold clock foisted on council retirees. "It will probably fetch a good price on EBay."

It turned out to be a clever move on my part to concede the offending clock was indeed an ugly eyesore that must be banished. Agreeing to its immediate conversion to cash proved a useful bartering tool, winning me the concession that my hoarded stash of souvenir restaurant and takeaway menus made the cut for the overseas trip, along with my prized collection of esoteric back scratchers.

Flying off to Greece for a two-week house hunting trip in the Mani, we left the key to the house with the estate agent who promised us that eager buyers were lining up to view. We were left a tad deflated upon receiving a call from said agent, flush with an offer that fell well below our monetary expectations. Apparently the rising damp was rising so rapidly it would soon join forces with the suspect stains that suggested something far more fatal than a supposed leaking roof, but the bidder was a builder willing to take on the project if we accepted his low-ball offer.

Marigold and I both saw eye to eye on the matter, realising if we didn't snap the hand off the potential buyer we could end up being stuck in Manchester indefinitely, not to mention living with the inconvenience of builders banging away from the murky depths below the floorboards to the pinnacle of the roof. Marigold shed a few tears when she realised the villa she'd been drooling over was now decidedly out of our price range, but she soon adjusted to the disappointment by declaring the premium price on seafront properties was a rip-off and we'd simply recommence our house hunting further inland. "Just think of the spectacular views we would enjoy from a mountain abode."

What followed was much traipsing around in the company of a foreign estate agent who flatly refused to accept our reduced budget was anything more than a bargaining tactic, insisting on showing us new build properties way beyond our price range. His persistence in presenting us with replica Mani towers soon paled when it finally dawned on him that we weren't the stinking rich foreigners he had assumed. He then shifted his focus to showing us dilapidated ruins that could be had for a song, presuming we were gullible enough to not realise such decrepit dwellings would require exorbitant expenditure to make then even remotely habitable. He enthused over properties that were little more than four tumbledown walls overrun with an impressive growth of weeds, and some worse-for-wear shacks invaded by goats. Constantly dropping the Greek word for potential, he assured us everything he showed us was rich in '*dynitikos*'. His use of the word was an annoyingly pretentious trait considering the agent Marigold had found online turned out to be Nordic rather than Greek.

Finally ditching the useless agent, we took refuge in a friendly taverna, opting for a table in the background shaded by some conveniently trailing bougainvillea. We could hide behind the ornamental climbing plant if the Nordic agent we hoped we had lost, suddenly popped into view. Marigold vented her frustration by kicking me sharply under the table when I voiced my natural concern about the state of the taverna kitchen, loudly reminding me I was pensioned off and no longer on duty. Her remark attracted the attention of a middle-aged Greek man at the next table who raised a questioning bushy eyebrow.

"My husband was a restaurant inspector," Marigold explained.

"Ah, the dream job, to be paid to eat," the man said, immediately getting the wrong end of the stick and introducing himself as Spiros. Marigold's second kick served as a warning that

BUCKET TO GREECE

I should just nod along and refrain from launching into an explanatory diatribe about the quality control standards of cleanliness I was accustomed to overseeing whilst working for the Food Standards Agency. The sudden appearance of the disgruntled Nordic stomping past the taverna, slowing to peer inside in pursuit of his lost property prey, caused Marigold to grab my arm and unceremoniously drag me under the table.

We waited with bated breath until Spiros laughingly informed us the coast was clear. Not shy about quizzing us about our involvement with that 'shyster house seller' he gave a knowing wink, saying "He have the bridge to sell you?" Over the next ten minutes Spiros entertained us with a scathing account of the agent's dubious business practices and his pretentious propensity for dropping mispronounced Greek words. Spiros' speech was amusingly punctuated with dramatic gesticulations, but his indisputable geniality shone through. We were delighted to make his acquaintance and, as luck would have it, Spiros just happened to have a house to sell us.

Chapter 3

Spiros has a House to Sell

Spiros' affable personality stood in marked contrast to that of the devious cold Nordic agent. We didn't feel he was trying to sell us a bridge when he confided he had recently inherited an old village house that had belonged to his uncle. Spiros explained the house needed modernising and he would much prefer to avoid any hassle with a quick cash sale.

"I am a humble man with no need of the two

houses. I honour the uncle's memory by only selling his house to the good people who will make it their home," Spiros said, offering to drive us to Meli for a viewing, insisting there was no time like the present.

"It wouldn't hurt to see it," I said to Marigold when Spiros told us the price. The house was such a bargain in comparison to the over-priced hovels the Nordic had dragged us round that there would be plenty of cash left over in the kitty for a touch of modernisation, providing Spiros hadn't exaggerated its habitable condition. Spiros' assurance that, "I throw in the dead uncle's furniture," convinced us that the house must at least have four fully formed walls and a roof to shelter said furniture from the elements.

Trusting our instincts, we assured Spiros we would be delighted to view his deceased uncle's house in Meli. Waiting for him to return with his vehicle, we were somewhat taken aback when he rolled up in a large black hearse. The tinted windows prevented us spotting the coffin in the back until we were safely ensconced in the cab. Spotting our slight unease, Spiros drew a heavy velvet curtain to conceal the backseat contents. He revealed he was the local undertaker and his recently departed uncle would no doubt enjoy the irony of a last visit to his home before he was buried the next morning.

"He die in the hospital, not the house," Spiros said, assuring us there were no morbid memories attached to the property.

Surprisingly, the hearse proved to be a very comfortable form of transport. Mindful of his dead uncle's presence, Spiros drove at a sedate pace, respectfully refusing to indulge in the Greek propensity for overtaking on hair-pin bends. The road we traversed swept up from the coastline, meandering through the hills and some picturesque out of the way villages offering spectacular views. Our excitement grew as we neared our destination and Spiros painted a delightful picture of the village of Meli. "Away from the maddening crowd of tourists you will breathe pure mountain air in the peace and tranquillity," Spiros gushed, selling us a honeyed dream.

Marigold clutched my hand when we passed the roadside sign announcing we had arrived in Meli, whispering "This could be it." The road narrowed considerably as we entered the village, a valley settlement lush with rich vegetation, dating back to Roman times. Stone houses with closed shutters hugged both sides of the road; decorative olive oil tins bursting with fragrant basil plants standing as pavement sentinels guarding quaint wooden doors.

"Hear how the quiet it is," Spiros said, just as a horn shattered the silence, patently ignoring the 'No Horns' road sign intended to preserve the peace of siesta time. The road was too narrow for two cars to pass, but Spiros refused to back-up to make way for the oncoming vehicle with its driver clamped angrily to the hooter. Both drivers stuck their heads out of their respective windows to engage in what we imagined to be choice Greek expletives accompanied by rude gestures, until the oncoming vehicle finally conceded to the hearse.

"Vangelis he not realise the uncle is in the back," Spiros explained, steering the hearse towards the charmingly cobbled village square where he parked up.

The frisson of excitement that gripped Marigold when she saw the house convinced me she was viewing it through rose-tinted glasses; it would fall on me to be the voice of sanity. The weather worn stones reflected the mellow early evening light and the blue wooden shutters embodied tradition. Spiros insisted we should see the roof terrace before stepping inside, enthusing the views at sunset were truly magnificent. Clutching the shaky balustrade we made our way up the rather hazardous stone steps to the rooftop where the panoramic vista of olive terraces bathed in the romantic sunset inclined towards the sea on the horizon.

The first thing that struck me was the delightful drop in temperature. It was such a hot humid day that my sweat soaked clothes stuck to every crevice of my body, and the delicately refreshing breeze was a most welcome relief.

"Please, not so close to the edge," Spiros advised, springing to Marigold's side. There were no walls or railings to interrupt the view before us, just the floor of the roof terrace tilting slightly towards a precipitous drop.

"Victor, could you ever imagine such a view? I can just picture us relaxing here on sunset evenings with a glass of wine. We could fill it with lanterns and Grecian urns bedecked with flowering plants."

"Don't forget the citronella candles," I reminded her, swatting away a blood-sucking mosquito.

Spiros had not exaggerated the wonderful views from the roof terrace, affording a three-hundred and sixty degree perspective of the sea, the village nestling in the footholds of the brooding slopes of Taygetos. Cautioning Marigold to steer clear of the edge, Spiros led her to the rear of the terrace, overlooking a sizeable overgrown garden. "See, there are fig, lemon and orange trees," he pointed out, artfully deflecting attention from the jungle of six-foot high weeds.

"And a very useful stone shed," I added, spotting a stone building off to one side of the garden.

"No, that is not part of the property, unless you can persuade the Guzim to sell it," Spiros said. "*Ela*, we look inside now."

Spiros kept up a running commentary extolling the house's good points. "It has three big bedrooms you could sleep in today, no work needed, though you must to use the imagination on the bathroom. But first I show you the palatial salon," he said grandly, ushering us into a huge room dimly illuminated by ornate glass chandeliers missing most of their bulbs. The room was flooded with light when Spiros dragged the thick blankets serving as curtains away from the windows, revealing a set of French doors opening onto a charming balcony overlooking the narrow pavement below.

My first impression was confused by the sheer amount of clutter. My attention was grabbed by an iron bedstead heaped with grubby blankets, huddled between a grease splattered two-ring hotplate and a massive American style refrigerator, shiny with new-ness. Spiros, spotting my confusion, explained, "My uncle he prefer to sleep in the kitchen," as though such an arrangement was patently nor-mal, making me curious to explore the three bedrooms.

A motley collection of mismatched taverna style chairs surrounded a large wooden table lit-tered with the detritus of what could well have been Spiros' uncle's last meal. At least the fish bones, olive pits and near empty bottle of ouzo indicated his last supper had been tasty. Spot-ting my interest, Spiros stalked over, filling three glasses with ouzo. Grabbing a fish skele-ton with some flesh and the head still attached, he hurled it over the balcony, saying, "The cats will make the fast work of that."

Downing the ouzo I took another look around the room. Gloomy Greek icons cluttered the mantle above an impressive fireplace. A makeshift aerial hanging from a metal coat hanger trailed down to a widescreen television, suspended at a precarious angle on the wall. Marigold honed in on a gaping hole in the cheap plasterboard covering the wall, exposing original stonework.

A rather grotesque concrete reproduction of a Greek god served as the base for a round slate table hosting a bowl of dusty plastic fruit. A garish gold framed mirror propped on top of an elegant mahogany dresser reflected a lurid pink and yellow floral velour sofa with a cheap wooden frame, the grey stuffing spilling out of the cushions and clashing with the bright green shag-pile bath mat serving as a rug. The bizarre mix of kitsch, dated and modern indicated Spiros' uncle was a man who had cared not a whit if his home decor was discordant.

Marigold could hardly contain her enthusiasm when Spiros rushed to unfurl a corner of the greasy linoleum floor covering, revealing a hidden treasure of beautiful decorative ceramic floor tiles in azure blue. Gushing over the authentic exposed stonework, the impressive high ceiling and the original tiles, Marigold's discerning eye could obviously see beyond the clutter and the peculiar assortment of furniture.

To my relief the main bedroom was a blank canvas since Spiros' dead uncle had dragged his bed into the kitchen. Spiros repeated the rigmarole of rolling back the nasty linoleum to reveal yet more stunning floor tiles in this and the remaining two bedrooms, both furnished with nothing more than bare mattresses. "See the quality of the built in wardrobes," Spiros said, blithely ignoring the fact they were patently cobbled together out of cheap MDF.

Marigold's face finally fell when we stuck our head round the bathroom door. Ugly brown tiles resembling sludge covered the walls and floor, held in place with murky mud coloured grout. A high on the wall toilet cistern dripped relentlessly into the foul stained toilet, and the shower was nothing more than a nozzle over a hole in the floor drain. A shambolic jumble of aftershave bottles and tins of boot polish adorned the top of the washing machine. Picking up a tin of shoe polish, Spiros said with a heartfelt sigh, "My uncle he always take the pride in his appearance."

"There's nothing like a well-polished shoe," I agreed.

"No, my uncle he use the shoe polish on the hair to cover the grey," Spiros clarified, adding, "I tidy these away in the bathroom cabinet."

Opening the door of the mirrored cabinet he swore under his breath when he discovered it was crammed full with tins of cat food. The awkward moment was interrupted by the ringing of Spiros' mobile and he excused himself to take the call on the roof where the reception was better.

"Victor, what do you think?" Marigold asked as soon as Spiros was out of earshot. I knew by the gleam in her eye that the question was superfluous, her mind already made up. "Use your imagination and picture the house free of clutter. It wouldn't take much to modernise it yet retain the original features. It really does appear to be of solid structure, most of the work needed is just cosmetic. Those floor tiles are an absolute find."

"The sludgy brown ones in the bathroom,"

I couldn't resist winding her up.

"Don't be so dense, Victor; nothing in that pit of a bathroom is salvageable." My quip that I was thinking of experimenting with the ready supply of shoe polish instead of Grecian 2000 earned me one of Marigold's withering looks.

"That disgrace of a bathroom will have to go and we'll need to fit a brand new kitchen, but the rest appears to be mainly cosmetic," she said, just as Spiros returned, ushering in the driver he had earlier engaged in a spot of road rage.

"I ask Vangelis to join us, he is local builder. It is good you talk with him about changes," Spiros said.

"I learn the English when doing renovation on many houses for foreigns," Vangelis explained. This immediately qualified him for the job in Marigold's eye; one of the problems she'd worried about was communicating with a builder whilst flicking through a phrase book.

Vangelis assured us the house was indeed solid. Readily agreeing it was in dire need of a new bathroom and kitchen, he offered to take us on a guided tour of the nearest town's bathroom showrooms. He told us he was a dab hand at fitting IKEA kitchens, removing cheap plaster-board, ripping up linoleum and digging deep holes if we were inclined to sink a swimming pool in the garden.

All the rooms we had explored were on the first storey of the house, accessed by an external stone stairway: I was keen to discover what lay below. Unfortunately Spiros didn't have a key to the ground floor door. The space was uncon-nected to the living area and was simply used for storage. "In old days the animals live in it, but I think the uncle store the old furniture and garden tools there," Spiros said, promising to lo-cate the key if we decided on a second viewing.

"It is the big space. You can do the many things with it," Vangelis said with an enigmatic wink.

"You have a lot to think on and tomorrow I bury the uncle," Spiros said solemnly before driving us back to the coast. Declining his offer to gate-crash the funeral we arranged to meet up in two days' time at the taverna where we first became acquainted.

Chapter 4

A Second Viewing

T he evening after viewing the house in Meli was spent in a pleasant coastal taverna, frantically scribbling calculations on the paper tablecloth, fingers greasy from the smeared residue of succulent lamb chops. I needed to ensure that if we took the plunge we wouldn't be reduced to sleeping on the grotty iron bedstead lurking in the kitchen.

Greece had just relinquished the drachma for the euro: the favourable exchange rate from sterling making us appear quite rich on paper. Selling up in England would leave us with ample funds to modernise the traditional village house and enjoy a comfortable standard of living. Even though the ground floor remained a mystery yet to explore, Marigold had fallen for the house. In truth, I didn't take much persuading to agree to a second viewing as the village of Meli held enormous appeal. I liked the idea of immersing ourselves in a small peaceful village rather than settling in a hot spot overrun with tourist throngs. My main hesitancy about moving to Greece had been coping with the heat, but the prevailing cool breeze of Meli was enticing, freeing me from the fear of pervasive mugginess. I felt it would be prudent to seize the opportunity before Marigold had another change of heart; her original vision of a coastal villa held less appeal to me and would definitely drain our coffers.

A gaggle of tourists adopting suitably mournful expressions and respectfully removing their sunhats made me feel like a fraud when Spiros pulled up at the taverna in his hearse, ready to whisk us off for our second viewing. Arriving at the house, Spiros pulled out a long rusty key which failed to fit the lock of the ground floor door. His exclamation of, "I'm such a clutch," left Marigold assuring him he wasn't a klutz at all and sympathising with the difficulties of being accurate in the foreign language he admitted he'd mastered by binge watching American movies with subtitles.

"I hope the uncle not have the key in the pocket," Spiros sighed, apologising profusely for the lack of access. Marigold and I grabbed the opportunity to explore Meli more fully whilst Spiros excused himself to go on a key hunt. We hoped it wouldn't involve digging his uncle up to rifle through his pockets.

The charmingly cobbled village square, shaded by plane trees, was dominated by a Byzantine church. Sprightly looking, weather-worn, elderly men sat outside the village shop, engaged in the game of Greek checkers known as *tavli*. Sipping from tiny porcelain cups of strong Greek coffee they eyed us warily from below furrowed brows, immediately breaking into beaming smiles when we bid them a hesitant good morning in the rudimentary Greek we had practised in the hearse with Spiros.

BUCKET TO GREECE

The interior of the village shop was a veritable Aladdin's cave, crammed with all the necessities of day-to-day life and an intriguing assortment of things we struggled to identify. Bunches of dried herbs that turned out to be mountain tea were strung above open sacks of dried beans. Tubs of plump purple marinated olives nestled next to salt encrusted anchovies and creamy blocks of feta cheese. There were huge pots of locally produced honey infused with thyme, and vast tubs of traditional Greek spoon sweets, quince, sour cherries, lemons and figs. Sold by weight they made a change from the more usual sealed jars, making us salivate at the prospect of tasting our way through each variety. Dusty bottles of the potent sweet red wine Mavrodafni vied for space on shelves packed with bottles of ouzo, raki and tsipouro. Tempted as we were by the novelty of prickly cactus fruit, we had no clue how to eat it, instead settling for two juicy peaches and two small bottles of water, cool with fridge condensation.

Ambling back to the house we gorged on the fruit. We were about to use the last of the water to wash the sticky peach juice from our fingers when a rake-thin old lady clad in traditional black widow's weeds gestured for us to stick our hands under her hosepipe. Gabbling at us in indecipherable Greek, her open friendliness was most welcoming. She smiled warmly as we repeated, "*Kalimera*," the Greek word for good morning, and hopelessly mispronounced "*Efcharisto*," the Greek word for thank you, unsure quite where to place the all-important stress accent. It struck me that a crash course in the Greek language would be vital if we were going to adapt and integrate into village life.

Luckily Spiros arrived to the rescue, picking the old lady up bodily and spinning her round, causing her to blush giddily. "You have met the Kyria Maria," he said, formally introducing us to what could be our new neighbour. "Kyria Maria is eighty-years-old and the mother of the village priest, Papas Andreas."

As Kyria Maria continued to speak Spiros served as translator, saying, "She is very pleased to meet you," adding in an unnecessary whisper as Maria knew no English, "She is glad to be rid of my uncle and welcome new neighbours. They fell out over some trivia twenty-years ago and have been drawing the daggers ever since."

Fascinated by the nature of a two-decade feud we bid good day to Maria whilst biting our tongues. We told Spiros it had been a delight to acquaint ourselves with the village shop. He tactfully refrained from mentioning that the shop kept peculiarly erratic hours, only opening when the owner was in the mood. He did fill us in on other local amenities, saying, "Dina at the taverna bakes the fresh bread for the village every Friday." He explained she used the traditional method of an outside wood oven to produce flat round loaves as big as a table. It was good to discover the village boasted a taverna that served only the freshest home grown products, but Spiros tactfully refrained from mentioning that the regular customer base primarily comprised ancient old men and the odd befuddled holidaymaker wandering too far from the tourist path.

Spiros had managed to locate a key to open the door to the ground floor of the house without being forced to dig up his uncle. The heavy wooden door creaked on its hinges, reluctantly opening to reveal a vast stone room with an arched ceiling. A single bare bulb dimly illuminated the space, crammed to bursting with garden tools, olive harvest implements and a motley collection of yet more dated furniture swathed in dense layers of cobwebs.

"Some foreigns have converted such spaces, but the house is so big you not need this, it is best used for the storage," Spiros suggested.

"And does everything in it come with the house?" I asked. Considering the neglected shambles of the garden I could make good use of the tools and hoped there might be the odd treasure Marigold could reclaim amongst the junk.

"Yes, the price we discuss is for the everything. We sort through, you can maybe furnish the empty rooms from what is here and I dispose of the rest," Spiros said optimistically. He was eager to sell the house quickly, wanting to invest the cash in an additional hearse that could double up as an illegal taxi if demand for its original purpose hit a dry spell.

"If we get rid of most of the junk this space will be excellent to store anything we bring over from England whilst the upstairs is modernised," Marigold said, pragmatic as ever. "It is an interesting space and we can always do something with it later."

BUCKET TO GREECE

Spotting a vast wooden barrel off to one side, I grew excited, presuming Spiros' uncle had used the space not only as a junk depository, but as a wine cellar. Spiros laughed at my assumption, explaining the barrel held his uncle's precious stash of extra virgin olive oil. Swinging the lid to one side he pulled on a rope, delicately levering a jug of oil to the surface. Marigold barely contained her delight that the house came complete with a good five hundred kilos of organic olive oil that Spiros assured us came from the last olive harvest. She eagerly accepted Spiros' offer to dip the unsavoury looking crust he magically produced from his pocket into the oily nectar for a tasting session. She sent a withering look in my direction when I declined due to my natural concern that the suspicious bread may be a breeding ground for possible pathogens picked up from Spiros' grubby pocket. Noting my crestfallen look that the barrel contained the juice of olives rather than grapes, Spiros declared the space was perfect for establishing my own wine cellar.

Our second viewing of the house in Meli afforded the opportunity to wander through the overgrown garden. In England my gardening duties had been limited to mowing the lawn and indiscriminately spraying weed killer, but the wilderness before me opened up endless possibilities: early retirement meant I would have plenty of time on my hands. Marigold gushed over the prospect of plucking fresh fruit from the trees and growing our own vegetables. Before she could get carried away with the idea of a pool, Vangelis fortunately joined us with a few rough calculations scratched on paper, gratifyingly far lower than I had anticipated.

His quotation included ripping the cheap plasterboard from the salon walls to expose the original stonework, removing the nasty linoleum and polishing up the floor tiles, and securing decorative railings around the roof terrace. The final price of the new bathroom and kitchen would be determined by the fittings we chose. Call us impetuous but there and then we told Spiros we would buy the house and avail ourselves of Vangelis' building skills. Vangelis assured us he would start on the bathroom as soon as we could bung him some money: this would ensure the house would be habitable by the time we made our move. Since the sale of our house in Manchester was progressing speedily in our absence we anticipated a quick flit once we returned to pack up our belongings, and sorted out our arrangements for travelling across Europe.

Hearty handshakes all round were interrupted by the arrival of Kyria Maria clutching a tray full of honey and walnut biscuits, a bottle of white wine and five glasses. Gesturing to the roof terrace, she gambolled up the hazardous stone steps with the sprightly agility of a mountain goat, to serve the refreshments. Unable to understand a single word she uttered, we smiled along jovially, delighted by such a warm neighbourly welcome. It was only many months later when I was able to converse in something more than rudimentary Greek that I realised Spiros hadn't offered a full translation, tactfully neglecting to mention Kyria Maria's presence had been prompted by her desire to see the exact spot where Spiros' uncle had plunged off the roof.

Chapter 5

New Found Friendships

The remainder of our two week house hunting trip to Greece flew by in a flurry of activity once Spiros accepted our offer on the house. He stalwartly guided us through the impenetrable obstacles of conducting legalities in a foreign language and accompanied us to offices where we were completely clueless, reduced to guessing what was going on. We nodded, smiled and signed on the dotted line in a daze when papers were presented

to us, and sighed in relief when the lawyer overseeing the house sale spoke impeccable English.

A small fortune was spent on mobile phone
calls arranging a transfer of funds from England
to cover the house deposit and the first tranche
of Vangelis' work. Even though we technically
couldn't claim full ownership of the house until
it was paid for in full, the National Bank of
Greece allowed us to open an account with
nothing more than a show of passports, our
newly claimed tax numbers, and our soon-to-be
address in Meli.

A haze of cigarette smoke surrounded the
rather unkempt and very casually dressed bank
manager who flatly refused to issue Marigold a
cheque book, waving his hands in frustration at
my wife's stubborn inability to accept cash was
king. She was naturally worried about carrying
large sums of cash on her person until Spiros reassured her that Meli was not exactly a hotbed
of international crime. The last recorded crime
in Meli was solved when a feral cat was exposed
as the guilty party responsible for stealing some
fish left unattended in a car, but the victim was
considered equally culpable for leaving the windows wound down. Marigold cheered up when

the bank manager promised to order her a cash point card and I agreed to always use a money belt instead of walking round with a wallet protruding from my back pocket.

The complexities of Greek bureaucracy would have been overwhelming without the calming presence of Spiros steering us through the process, between funerals. Spiros was fascinated by Marigold's observation that visiting the bank was just like hanging around at the delicatessen counter in Tesco, waiting for one's number to come up. He immediately invited himself on a visit to England to "check out the Tesco" until we pointed out we were about to up-sticks to Greece. No such ticketing system was in place at the tax office which operated more on the lines of an unruly scrummage. Burly moustached men elbowed their way to the counter, indiscriminately interrupting and loudly demanding attention, but they were no match for Spiros who could scrum with the best of them.

In contrast the lawyer's office was an oasis of calm. Our legal advisor calmly talked us through the standard procedure of bunging half the cost of the house to Spiros in used notes: on paper we would only pay the objective value of the house, thus reducing the transfer tax. Spiros promised to assist us when it came time to transfer the electricity, water and telephone line to our names once we were officially resident in Greece, and to accompany us to the police station to obtain the residency permits we would require to purchase a left-hand drive car. Nothing appeared to be too much trouble to Spiros in his role as our self-appointed guardian sponsor. Although we were paddling out of our depth with all the legalities we allowed ourselves to be swept along, confident in Spiros' steadying presence.

With all the legal stuff out of the way, Vangelis finally took us to town on our final day, treating us to a whirlwind tour of shops full of bathroom fittings. Marigold was in her element selecting sky blue tiles to replace the current sludge. Choosing a brand new bathroom suite comprising a low level flush toilet, a pedestal washbasin, and a modern shower cubicle, she offered a nervous laugh when Vangelis pointed out the new vanity unit offered ample storage space for cat food and shoe polish. Putting her foot down, Marigold refused to countenance the purchase of a bath, complaining she'd had, "Thirty-five years of scrubbing away your tidemark and from now on you can make do with showers." Her additional argument that showering conserved water was pretty feeble considering she'd been hinting about splashing out on a swimming pool.

Marigold cajoled Vangelis into making a stop at a large furniture store. She was keen to see what was available; it would help her decide if we needed to bring furniture over from England or should simply buy new on arrival. She had already determined the resident pink and yellow floral velour sofa, in all its repulsive glory, would have to go, its actual comfort factor doing nothing to mitigate its ugliness. I could only look on in amusement when Marigold's jaw dropped to the floor upon discovering the furniture store was stuffed to the gills with identical floral sofas. Her comment that she would never give house room to something so tasteless proved terribly tactless when Vangelis revealed the exact same sofa held pride of place in his living room.

Before heading back, Vangelis suggested a detour to the nearest supermarket, his wife having instructed him to bulk buy packets of frozen octopus on special offer. Wandering the aisles Marigold became excited. "Oh look Victor, they sell W..." she shouted, pointing to a particular brand of cat food that shall remain nameless. "It was always my favourite," she added, referring wistfully back to her days as a pet food taster and throwing four tins of the stuff into Vangelis' trolley.

It was futile to point out to Marigold that we had no cats since her purchase was obviously sentimental; it seemed to reassure her to know she would be able to find familiar products in this foreign land where the tea came in twig form and the fruit needed an instruction manual. Vangelis insisted on paying for the cat food along with the octopus, happily assuring Marigold the four tins would be waiting for her in the new vanity unit in our newly revamped bathroom when we returned to Greece.

By the time Vangelis delivered us back to our apartment it was early evening as we'd made several pit stops for coffee. Vangelis appeared incapable of functioning without an hourly shot of caffeine, accompanied by a cheese pie. We were expecting Spiros to drive down to join us for dinner and we persuaded Vangelis to let us treat him too. Waiting for Spiros to arrive we chatted over drinks in the usual taverna, the octopus defrosting in the back of Vangelis' pick-up alongside our new toilet. Marigold, always eager to devour the latest gossip, prised the information from Vangelis that Spiros had only recently learned our language in order to impress an English woman who had settled in Meli. Shrugging his shoulders Vangelis revealed, "Spiros is single and hope to impress her with his big car." His observation amused me as I couldn't imagine Spiros' hearse exactly serving as a babe magnet.

Marigold was delighted to learn we wouldn't be the only foreigners in Meli. Curious about the other inhabitants of the village we discovered that in addition to the woman who had caught Spiros' fancy, there were a few other houses owned by fellow Brits. "Meli is very Euro centric," Vangelis told us, explaining that as well as comprising a population of Greeks and Albanians, Meli had attracted foreign retirees from Germany, Italy and Belgium. I immediately decided that once I became a Greek resident I would embrace my new status and declare myself a proud European rather than British.

Spiros' arrival in the hearse piqued our curiosity; he had an attractive female companion with him. Immediately jumping to the assumption that the heavily made up pleasantly plump woman he was with must be the English woman he was trying to impress with his newly acquired language skills, I reconsidered my views on the pulling power of hearses. I was taken by surprise when the woman immediately honed in on Vangelis, slapping him round the head before dragging him away from the table. At this point in our acquaintance Spiros had taken to double kissing Marigold and smothering me in a manly embrace ending in a vigorous back slap. On this occasion I staggered from his grasp, choking on the overpowering cloying scent of cheap cologne; it struck me that Spiros had been helping himself to his dead uncle's washing machine collection of aftershave.

Spiros slapped down our interest in his budding romance by explaining Athena was Vangelis' wife. She had spotted the frozen octopus melting in the back of his pick-up as soon as the hearse pulled up. The shame faced Vangelis soon reappeared, staggering under the weight of the dripping packets his wife implored the taverna owner to stash in his freezer while we dined. Vangelis returned to the table sporting a damp patch on his shirt. The dark smudge that appeared when the wet patch dried led me to surmise Vangelis had followed Spiros' uncle's example and had been experimenting with shoe polishing his visibly greying chest hair.

A sharp kick under the table from Marigold stopped me in my tracks when I started to warn Vangelis about the health hazards of re-freezing fish products that had been allowed to defrost in the heat. Vangelis' wife joined the table, planting an enormous smacker on the head she had so recently slapped, and introductions were made. Athena's English was as limited as our Greek, so once again Spiros and Vangelis were roped in to translate.

Athena wasted no time in insisting that as soon as we moved into the house in Meli we must join them for a home cooked meal of octopus marinated in oil and vinegar. Whilst eager to fraternise with our new neighbours, I was appalled at the prospect of voluntarily eating my way to food poisoning. Diplomatically inventing an octopus allergy to let me off the hook, in the hope Athena would instead offer to cook something less inclined to inflict botulism through irresponsible freezing methods, proved a self-defeating move. I spent the rest of the evening unable to indulge in the delicious grilled octopus Spiros ordered for the table.

After much intrusive badgering by Athena, Spiros revealed he had invited Cynthia, the English woman he was crushing on, to join us this evening. He didn't appear too dejected by her rejection since her excuse that her cat was about to produce kittens sounded plausible, and she had after all turned out for his uncle's funeral. Spiros hadn't had much luck with the ladies; he blamed his failure to win hearts on a natural female squeamishness to dating a man who associated so closely with corpses.

Vangelis and Athena had been happily married for almost three decades and were grateful that the influx of foreigners to the area kept Vangelis busy with building work. They had encouraged their two grown sons to go off to university, leading to them both landing professional roles in Athens, but visiting home at every opportunity. Many Meli residents under pensionable age had been forced to move out of the area in search of work. They told us that nearly half of the houses in Meli were owned by Greeks working in big cities, only enjoying the chance to visit their home village during the holidays or for mandatory voting.

Our dinner companions were eager to learn more about us. We readily revealed we had been married for thirty-five years, but elusively skirted round the details of our actual first encounter, simply admitting we had met in a shop. We didn't like to divulge that we had met in a branch of B & Q, both desperate to get our hands on the last galvanised bucket on sale. I'd planned to snap up the bucket to use as a novelty beer cooler whilst Marigold wanted to use it as a decorative hanging feature for flowers. As we fought over the bucket I was distracted by Marigold's beauty. Instantly captivated by her flowing Titian hair and smouldering green eyes as deep as rock pools, I relinquished my claim on the galvanised steel receptacle in exchange for the promise of a first date. We were married just five months later: the bucket of blooming begonia suspended over our new front door clipped my forehead sharply when I carried my blushing bride over the threshold.

No matter how hard I tried to block out my ignominious start in life, happenstance seemed determined to chuck freak moments at me that hankered back to my bucket beginnings: I learnt to interpret such chance moments as serendipity. Bucket coincidences have continued to crop up throughout my life. Five years earlier I had the misfortune to break an arm whilst holidaying in Patmos. Our son Benjamin dropped everything and rushed over to help Marigold struggle back with the luggage on the ferry. On the bucket flight home from Athens he experienced a serendipitous moment, meeting the air steward Adam who is now his life-partner. Still, such topics were not for public consumption since Marigold remains as sensitive to any mention of buckets as she does to talk of the clap.

The evening was a great success. Even though Athena was obviously younger than us, she exuded a motherly air, promising to take Marigold under her wing and introduce her to village life. Officially retired from her dangerous occupation of hairdressing due to the government decreeing it involved exposure to hazardous hairspray, she offered perms, colour rinses and blow-dries in her kitchen. Marigold got a bit huffy when Athena offered to touch up her roots; she'd always been a natural red head and was a bit sensitive to her recent reliance on colour out of a bottle.

Vangelis blustered that learning Greek would be easy since so many English words originated from Greek ones. Pressing his point, he enunciated slowly and precisely, teaching us the Greek words for salad, tomato and soup. It was true they were remarkably easy to master as they were almost identical to the English versions.

As the evening came to a close Spiros reminded us that the next time we'd be in Greece we would no longer be holidaymakers but actual Greek residents. Vangelis promised to crack on with ripping out the grotty bathroom and installing the new one. Our imminent move was toasted with generous glasses of Metaxa, and I proposed a hearty toast to new found friendships I genuinely hoped would last a lifetime.

Chapter 6

Just Three Weeks to Greece

I certainly won't miss this weather," Marigold said, bracing to step from the aeroplane into the Manchester drizzle, shivering in the strappy sundress so unsuitable to the inclement conditions we'd flown back to. Raiding the suitcases the moment they appeared on the carousel, she made a grab for a cardigan, only to discover the bottle of ouzo she'd wrapped inside it to prevent breakage had leaked all over the cashmere. The stench was so overpowering we were forced to drive home with the car windows down, despite the drizzle having morphed into teeming rain. How I longed for a bottle of Spiros' dead uncle's aftershave to mask the boozy reek of alcohol. I hoped we wouldn't be pulled over by the boys in blue since there was no way the cardigan would pass a breathalyser. By the time we arrived on the doorstep our clothes were so soggy we had to wring them out, leaving puddles of watered down ouzo in our wake. We were in no mood to deal with the estate agent lurking furtively in the porch, pretending he just happened to be passing.

The ouzo aroma clinging to us probably convinced him we would be a drunken pushover for the offer he was waiting to spring on us. The builder buyer, suddenly eager to take early possession of our house, was prepared to up his original offer by four thousand pounds if we would agree to vacate the premises in just three weeks instead of the previously agreed two months.

Marigold immediately said it was quite impossible: we faced the enormous task of packing all our worldly possessions and saying goodbye to family and friends. Telling the estate agent to stay put in the porch, out of earshot, I pulled my wife indoors. The sum mentioned was not trivial and would go a fair way towards Marigold's dream kitchen.

"But Victor, three weeks, it's no time at all," she protested.

"He's a cash buyer and there's no chain. Neither of us is working so it's ample time to stuff our belongings into packing boxes," I argued, persuasively adding, "The extra money is not to be sniffed at."

"But Victor, three weeks," she continued to argue.

"Okay, we'll decline the offer and risk losing the buyer. You can make do with that grotty two-ring cooker, I'm sure it won't take you too long to scrub it free from grease," I countered.

Our argument was interrupted by the estate agent letting himself in through the back door and upping the buyers's offer by an additional thousand pounds.

"We'll take it," I stated firmly, putting my foot down before Marigold could object and escorting the pushy agent out by the scruff of his neck.

Marigold's reluctance to immediately snap the estate agent's hand off was born of sudden doubt. Away from the lure of Greece she'd begun to question if we were doing the right thing in up-sticking to a foreign country. I thought her sudden dithering a bit rich considering she'd been the one so set on selling up and moving to Meli.

"But are we doing the right thing?" she asked. "Benjamin may feel abandoned."

"Get a grip Marigold. Benjamin is not a helpless child; he is thirty-five years old. It won't be any more inconvenient for him to visit us in Greece than it is for him to drive up the M1 in a traffic jam, and I'm sure he'll appreciate the free holidays. If we back out now we will lose the deposit we paid to Spiros and we can't expect a refund on the bathroom suite since we paid cash to avoid the VAT."

"I'm sorry Victor, I'm just being silly. Of course I want to move to Greece, but three weeks makes it sound so sudden, so final."

"It's better than putting up with two more months of this dismal weather; wouldn't you rather be relaxing on our new roof terrace in the heat?" I pointed out. "And you'll be able to keep a beady eye on the renovations if we're actually there. I'll order some packing boxes tomorrow and we can invite Benjamin and Adam to spend a weekend with us before we leave. Give Barry a ring, fingers crossed he has a free slot in three weeks."

Marigold's brother Barry just happened to own a removals company and had already offered to put himself and a van at our disposal for an international flit. By a stroke of good fortune he was not only free to drive us and our worldly possessions to Greece, but promised to stay on for a few days to help us settle in.

Barry also agreed to take charge of selling our cars on our behalf once we were out of the country. We didn't want to go through the rigmarole of driving them to Greece and then popping over the nearest border every six months to comply with the ludicrous regulations on British number plates.

Chapter 7

Coals to Newcastle

Having already bid goodbye to my colleagues at the Food Standards Agency I had plenty of free time on my hands to get on with the packing. Decisions were made over which furniture to take with us and which electrical appliances were worth carting across Europe on the off-chance they could cope with the dodgy looking two-pronged circuits.

My meticulous packing method involved

putting our possessions into two distinct piles: one to come with us and one to dispose of. The bulk of this work fell on my shoulders since Marigold spent most of her time enjoying farewell lunches with friends and scouring the shops for new outfits that would be suitable for warmer climes. She would then return home to pass judgement on my piles.

"Victor, don't you think there's already enough junk in the new basement without importing more of your rubbish," she exclaimed. Casting a derisory eye over my collection of well-thumbed manuals on the subject of kitchen hygiene, refrigerator rules and food borne pathogens, as though they had no more merit than old toe nail clippings, she began to stuff them into a charity shop bag. Holding the kitchen hairnet I had worn in my professional capacity disdainfully at arm's length, she rolled her eyes, saying, "Victor, you will never need this again. You must accept your days of poking round in restaurant kitchens are over."

"I suppose so," I reluctantly agreed, grabbing the hairnet and throwing it into the charity bag.

Marigold immediately retrieved it. "Victor

even the charity cases would turn their nose up at a second hand hairnet, go and put it in the dustbin for goodness sake." Of course she was only trying to get me out of the way so she could immediately retrieve the bundle of moving abroad books I had previously relegated to the disposal pile.

We had several discussions about what to do, if anything, with the ground floor portion of the house in Meli. I was quite relieved that Marigold didn't appear to have grandiose plans for the space that would involve investing a big chunk of our savings. Marigold was quite relieved that there was no internal staircase, declaring it would be a godsend to have a house on one floor should we possibly develop dodgy hips when we hit old age. I pointed out that the living space was indeed on one floor, but we would still need to climb the exterior stairs to reach it, not to mention the hazardous stone steps leading up to the roof terrace. She shot me down with a stern, "I'm sure they are perfectly capable of installing stair lifts in Greece whenever our hips start creaking enough to dictate we need one."

Every day Marigold voiced new objections

to the personal items I chose to take with me, endlessly reminding me we couldn't possibly take everything with us. We had a rare marital argument over my model railway collection when Marigold accused me of being "a bit past it to still be playing with toy trains," denouncing my reaction as 'sniffy' when I pointed out my miniature replicas were valuable collectibles. At the same time she had a hard time parting with her own personal possessions, indeed sabotaging my efforts to trim down our belongings by adding to them daily.

Panicking that we may not be able to readily purchase our favourite foods in Greece, she dragged me to Tesco, throwing random items into a trolley. I looked on in amazement when jars of Marmite joined her stash of Colman's mustard and Tetley teabags, since neither of us could stand the salty yeast paste.

"I've read that Marmite is a natural mosquito deterrent and you know how attractive the pesky blood-suckers find you," Marigold explained.

"I refuse to walk round covered in Marmite," I protested.

"Oh Victor, you don't rub it in, you eat it,"

Marigold scoffed.

"I'd rather be bitten alive by the blighters than eat that muck," I retorted.

"You may think differently when you are covered from head to toe in itchy red blotches," she shot back. "Anyway, we may well have guests over who like the foul stuff, so it won't go to waste."

I took an instant loathing to the random Marmite guzzling guests likely to invade our new Greek home when Marigold used them as an excuse to object to my stockpiling tins of Fray Bentos steak and kidney pies. Apparently their inclusion in our kitchen cupboards would mark us down as some kind of culinary peasants. Not only were they likely to sneer at my choice of bake-in-the-tin suppers, but they were already demanding the very best Tesco bed linen. Marigold just tutted when I suggested we could purchase sheets for the spare bedroom at some distant point in the future. She continued to pile the trolley high with all manner of things she wasn't sure if we could buy in Greece, finally allowing me the concession of one solitary bottle of Heinz salad cream.

BUCKET TO GREECE

Marigold's absolute insistence that we export two cats from Manchester to set up house with us in Greece left me totally baffled, once again shaking my head at the warped ways in which my wife's brain seemingly operates. "It's like taking coals to Newcastle. It's not as if Greece is short on cats of its own," I argued futilely.

Marigold's absolute stance would have at least made sense if we'd had any actual cats to begin with, but our Manchester home had always been a blessedly pet free zone. Marigold had always wanted a few feline friends, but fretted they would cause havoc whilst we were out at work. She almost gave in to temptation many times, only to have panic attacks at the thought of the mischief they might create whilst having the run of the place. Her fears were exacerbated by her fetish for watching online cat videos, a particular cat-brained habit, featuring cuddly felines ripping their way through toilet rolls and risking electrocution by chewing their way through random wires.

I tried to convince Marigold there was no point in importing her imaginary cats, since Greece was teeming with the creatures. I pointed out the particular unhygienic practice of cats having the run of tavernas and suggested she simply grab a cute one while we were dining out and smuggle it home in her handbag. She was utterly aghast at the idea, adamant that any cat which came to live with us would be of suitable pedigree and purchased from a reputable pet shop, something Greece seemed to be lacking in.

With just three weeks to the move, Marigold purchased two cats of somewhat dubious pedigree and arrived home covered in scratches. This was the calamitous result of attempting to cram Catastrophe and Clawsome (naturally the two furry additions have earned their own aliases) into uncomfortable looking travel baskets they had no truck with. Marigold had imprisoned the cats in baskets to take them straight from the pet shop to the vets. They needed rabies shots and health certificates before they could travel.

As anyone with half a brain could have predicted the two new arrivals created havoc amidst the endless supply of packing boxes, in addition to the extra complication of needing their very own travel passports at great expense. The cats were the final straw. Determined to put

a stop to my wife's extravagance I put my foot
down, taking the scissors to her credit card.

Chapter 8

Indian Spices

There was much to pack into the three weeks before we emigrated, in addition to actual packing. I compiled neat folders of every random bit of paperwork we may need to get our hands on in the future, penned numerous Change of Address cards, and carefully labelled all the boxes with colour coded stickers. Utility companies were informed we would no longer require their services and final cheques were popped in the post after accurate meter readings were recorded.

As our final weekend in England dawned Marigold brimmed with excitement, anticipating the arrival of Benjamin and his life partner Adam. The two boys were just the muscle we needed to help Barry and I load the boxes into the removal van. Whilst Marigold beautified herself up for their visit with a trip to the hairdresser, I was interrupted by the arrival of the builder buyer, barging in and demanding he needed to do an urgent damp calculation. He proved to be a bumptious type, strutting through the house insulting our decor and questioning the wisdom of our move to foreign parts.

Clutching a damp meter he prostrated himself on the living room carpet, muttering, "Greece," to the skirting board. His scathing tone suggested a horror of venturing any further afield than the local bus route.

"That's a bit too foreign for my taste. You'd be better off in Spain, at least it's full of Brits. The wife's always going on about us having a holiday in Spain because she fancies a tan, but I can't be doing with all that foreign food so I bought her a sun bed."

"So you're not a fan of tapas and paella?"

"What's that mate? The taps, no I don't need to check them today, just the damp."

"No, not taps, tapas. I was referring to Spanish food," I corrected him, wondering why I was bothering to make conversation with this culinary troglodyte.

"No time for it mate, I like proper British food. You can't beat a good curry. Speaking of which, it's Friday. Me and the wife get a takeaway every Friday from the Spice Bucket. You can't beat their vindaloo," he said, shuffling into the kitchen.

Mention of the Spice Bucket made me wince in genuine horror since I was painfully familiar with the slovenly kitchen habits practiced there. I'd been forced to award them a pitiful 'one' on the FSA score board. The number wasn't low enough to shut them down, but it was low enough to make me shudder at the thought of eating anything emanating from the kitchen that would be more aptly named the Slime Bucket. The proprietor, Mr Chowdhury, proudly blue-tacked the official rating on his grubby door: struggling with English comprehension he mistook the number one for a first place prize in the takeaway stakes.

Professional restraint prevented me from warning our house buyer about the dangers of dabbling in dodgy curries from less than pristine kitchens. Eager to be rid of him, I ignored the polite norm of offering a cuppa, keen to crack on with the last of the packing before the boys arrived. The frantic beeping of the damp meter attracted Clawsome to investigate, initiating a series of violent sneezes from the builder, who wheezed, "You didn't tell me you had cats. I'm allergic. I'll have to wait until they've moved out to finish my damp checking."

"They are a very recent addition to our household," I explained, watching him scarper speedily through the back door, happy that Marigold's hasty feline purchase had served some useful purpose.

"You'd best make sure you give the place a good hovering before you leave to get rid of all the cat hairs," the buyer gasped, struggling for breath on the patio. Relieved to have put some distance between himself and the toxic cat hairs, he slowly recovered his composure. Stretching out a perspiring hand to shake, he reminded me to be sure we were out of the house by first thing

Monday. He bid me goodbye with a cheery, "Right then mate, good luck in Greece."

Dashing indoors I rifled desperately through the packed boxes, trying to recall which one housed my industrial supply of hand sanitizer. Glad to be free of his perspiring germs, I rewarded Clawsome with a tin of salmon before scrubbing the skirting board with neat bleach.

Marigold was in her element fussing over Benjamin and Adam. Unfortunately she was unable to treat them to a home cooked meal since all the plates and pans were in sealed boxes, so I booked a table at our favourite Indian restaurant. Always mindful of the dangers of contracting a nasty bout of food poisoning when dining out, I had every confidence in my choice of the Bhilai Bhaji. It rightfully deserved the highest accolades for cleanliness, scoring top marks in all areas of health code compliance, in addition to serving the most deliciously piquant sour lemon pickle.

Entering the Bhilai Bhaji that evening Marigold said, "Thank goodness our move to Greece will put paid to all your tiresome restaurant restrictions," voicing her annoyance that our dining out choices were limited to establishments that had professionally passed my exacting hygiene standards. She had long harboured the delusion that my career as a health inspector was a natural stepping stone to the more prestigious profession of restaurant critic, failing to understand my training left me naturally reluctant to risk eating anywhere that I didn't have intimate knowledge of the sanitary practices employed. I'd always felt incredibly fortunate that my job didn't require me to actually taste test any food from the kitchens I inspected. Marigold would have considered it a perk of the job, but then again she has much laxer standards and her palate has been ruined by years of sampling pet food.

"Dad has every right to be cautious where he dines, considering some of the vile things he has uncovered," Benjamin defended. Since childhood he had lapped up my tales of kitchen gore with relish, delighting in the most disgusting revelations of green chicken, eruptions of mould sprouting from rotting vegetables, and the hidden horrors lurking below the surface of scummy sauces. Naturally I embellished some of my accounts to amuse him, not realising it would leave him with a life-long phobia of restaurant chips. To this day he flinches at the very suggestion of ordering French fries in public, convinced some penny pinching chef has likely filched the rejects from the plate of a spit happy customer and merrily lobbed them back into the deep-fat fryer.

"Well, your Dad will have to get used to eating in places where he hasn't snooped in the kitchens first, once we move," Marigold said. "He was quite adventurous when we were over there house hunting."

It was true I was always much more reckless about dining out on holiday, even though it required me to venture outside my comfort zone, primarily because Marigold put her foot down and refused to cook. The holiday mood made it much easier for Marigold to persuade me to enter unknown taverna territory; unless a place looked so suspiciously grubby it set off my inbuilt cockroach detector.

"Greek food tends to be freshly cooked each day, there is less reliance on re-heating premade dishes that have been stored at dubious temperatures," I pontificated.

"I found a new website that should be right

up your alley," Adam volunteered, tucking into a fragrant plate of aloo gobi. "You can post online reviews about restaurants. There shouldn't be a conflict of interest as you're no longer checking out kitchens professionally."

"That sounds perfect Victor, you could turn it into a nice little hobby," Marigold patronisingly pronounced. "If you focused a bit more on the food it might stop you obsessing about how often the kitchen floor is disinfected."

My wife's sarcasm was like water off a duck's back as I was so accustomed to accusations of being obsessive. I took pride in my role of being a grand stalwart against filth and botulism, protecting not only my family but much of Greater Manchester.

As we made room on the table for some stuffed potato parathas Benjamin presented me with the gift of a handy Greek phrase book, laughingly saying, "I'm not sure you'll find this one very useful, but it will definitely amuse you."

"I'm sure any phrase book will prove beneficial in my efforts to get a grasp on the Greek language," I countered, thumbing through the pages with interest. "Hmm, I see your point

Benjamin. Since it is September, a time of year when Greece is inclined to be sunny, I probably won't need to get the hang of this tongue twister just yet: 'Where can I buy a pair of galoshes and a matching umbrella?' Still, it's very handy to know that the Greek word for umbrella is *ombrela*, nice and easy to remember."

Adam advised me to discover as many Greek words as possible that mirrored their English counterparts, saying it would be a great way to immediately and impressively increase my Greek vocabulary. His advice reminded me of Vangelis' assurance that many English words originated from Greek ones.

"This one could be useful if we ever branch into livestock: 'I have a pig for sale,'" I said, reading aloud from the phrase book.

"Don't talk such nonsense, we are not keeping pigs," Marigold snapped crossly. She had already reacted negatively to my suggestion that we keep chickens. I found her excuse that the imaginary chickens would terrify her cats quite lame when it was patently obvious her objection to chickens was their barnyard smell and indiscriminate droppings.

"Will you be able to get Indian food in the

Mani?" Benjamin asked, tactfully changing the subject.

"All the restaurants seem to specialise in Greek food," Marigold said, looking suddenly worried her culinary choices could be limited. "I suppose if we want something different, such as Chinese, Thai or Indian, we'll have to cook it ourselves."

"But will you be able to get the ingredients easily?" Adam asked.

"Get the bill Victor," Marigold demanded across our half-eaten dinner, a horrified expression on her face as she realised she'd forgotten to bulk buy something so vital. "We must do a mad dash to Tesco and a midnight run to Chinatown to stock up on spices before they close."

Chapter 9

Moving Countries

Benjamin and Adam helped Barry and I load the furniture and boxes into the removal van, whilst Marigold busied herself vacuuming up every last trace of cat, mindful of our buyer's debilitating allergy. Marigold sobbed sentimentally over our flit, shedding tears as we hugged the boys' farewell and exchanged goodbyes with the neighbours. It all turned into a bit of an anti-climax. Everyone gathered to wave us off, but our departure was then delayed by another hour since Marigold hadn't anticipated the sight of the travel baskets would reduce the cats to a state of frantic panic. They mewlingly objected to any suggestion of driving across the continent in cages by rushing into hiding. By the time we finally trapped the cats and loaded them into the van our neighbours had all grown bored and wandered off, and the boys had driven away, desperate to avoid any traffic snarl-ups on the M1.

My pragmatic approach of luring the cats into their baskets with a tempting offer of catnip proved folly in hindsight since it drove the them crazy all the way to the Channel Tunnel. This necessitated a stop off at a Folkestone veterinarian for some cat calming sedatives, causing us to miss our scheduled Euro Shuttle. A state of drugged bliss ensured the cats were calm from Folkestone to the Swiss border, with only Barry's violent bouts of travel sickness interrupting our smooth drive through France, an occupational hazard he'd been unable to shake even through extensive hypnosis and electroshock treatment.

When we finally arrived in Brindisi to catch the ferry to Patras we had been on the road for four days, breaking our journey with overnight stays at cat friendly hotels where Barry slept off the drowse inducing side effects of his inefficacious travel sickness medication. Luckily the crossing proved calm, sparing Marigold and I the terrible seasickness which plagued Barry and the cats. Barry looked decidedly green when we embarked on the final stretch of our journey, the road trip from Patras to Meli, so we left him to sleep off his biliousness in the van whilst Marigold and I enjoyed a coastal lunch break of grilled fresh prawns, toasting our arrival in Greece with a glass of chilled wine.

It was late afternoon by the time the removal van negotiated Meli's narrow main street. We were forced to interrupt Spiros' siesta since his hearse was in the only parking space large enough to accommodate the van. Barry attempted to park the van outside the house but it immediately blocked all access through the village, prompting Spiros to round up a production line of village men to assist in carrying our belongings from the village square. Considering Barry is a professional removal man he proved as much use as a chocolate teapot in actually moving anything, so green around the gills he was forced to lie down in the shade of an ancient plane tree sipping lemonade. Still, he had done a sterling job of steering the unwieldy removal van across Europe whilst riddled with motion sickness, and deserved a well-earned rest.

Our new neighbour, eighty-year-old Kyria Maria, put Barry to shame, grabbing a huge cardboard box full of essential spices and scuttling up the hazardous stone steps with goat-like agility. Marigold was reduced to miming her displeasure when she caught Maria rifling through the box with as much enthusiasm as if she had first dibs on the offerings at the local bring-and-buy sale. Spiros directed his line of volunteers with the aplomb of an orchestra conductor, pointing to the ground floor storage space or the steps to the living quarters, on Marigold's say so. I couldn't help but notice that most of the volunteers appeared older than me, yet physically fitter. Wondering if this could be down to their healthy Greek diet, I contemplated adopting it with gusto, perhaps binning the secret stash of Fray Bentos pies I had managed to sneak past Marigold's prying eyes.

I rewarded each of the village helpers with a crisp twenty euro note, much impressed with their no nonsense approach to mucking in so readily. The cash was received with sturdy back slaps and much repetition of the word *tipota* which Spiros translated as 'nothing.' I thought that was a bit rich considering it was actually twenty euros apiece, until Spiros embellished his translation to explain they actually meant 'think nothing of it.'

"*Yassou* friends," Vangelis hollered from the roof terrace, beckoning us to join him. Surrounded by the detritus of discarded frappe cups and remnants of cheese pie crusts, he was hard at work securing the final section of decorative railings. We admired the choice of ornately scrolled railings, an elegant addition to the roof terrace, and decided to leave the choice of paint colour until later.

We remained blissfully ignorant the railings had been a rush job, ordered by Spiros to prevent a repeat of his uncle's near deadly plunge from the roof. His crafty habit of dodging pertinent translating kept us in the dark about his uncle's fate for another month. When we finally learned that his uncle had died from falling off the roof after imbibing too much ouzo, Spiros reiterated his assertion that his relative had died in the hospital. He'd just neglected to mention the hospital death had followed closely on from the broken body being scraped off the pavement outside the house. About to accept Vangelis' challenge to test the railings ability to prevent us from plummeting from the roof, Spiros cut him off short, suggesting we follow him down to inspect the progress made indoors.

The new bathroom suite, installed in the newly tiled bathroom, was a triumph, the room transformed to an airy light space retaining no trace of its former sludge. The low level toilet met with Marigold's approval and she declared it ensured the house was immediately habitable. The sight of the four tins of cat food facetiously placed in the new bathroom cabinet reminded us that the cats were still caged up in the depths of the removal van and needed to be introduced to their new home.

Vangelis told us that the large plastic sheet suspended from the ceiling of the grand salon was intended to separate the kitchen area from the yet to be modernised living area, now mercifully free of junk and clutter but concealed under a covering of dust sheets. Pushing through the plastic barrier, excited to see what progress had been made on the new kitchen, Marigold's face fell flat when she discovered the only thing remotely kitchen-like in the kitchen area was Spiros' uncle's massive American style refrigerator.

"I hate to be critical Vangelis, but a usable kitchen would have been more useful than decorative railings on the roof terrace," Marigold pointed out, perplexed by his priorities.

"I do the kitchen next, but safety was paramount considering what happened to Pedros," Vangelis replied.

"Marigold, your choice of kitchen was too important to leave to us men," Spiros interrupted before we had chance to enquire who Pedros was and what fate had befallen him.

"Of course, I didn't think," Marigold apologised, belatedly realising she shouldn't have expected a kitchen to be in place when she hadn't actually chosen one.

"We can shop for a kitchen tomorrow," Vangelis promised, adding, "At least you can make coffee." I noticed the traditional Greek *briki* used for brewing coffee on top of the grease splattered old hotplate, next to a packet of powdered Bravo. The hotplate had been relegated to the floor when the gloomy old dark cabinets and worktop had been ripped out.

"The important thing is you have the toilet to flush and a good place to sleep, the rest we do tomorrow," Spiros said, dragging us into the master bedroom. The vile linoleum floor covering had been removed and the original ceramic tiles restored to full glory. The nasty MDF built-in wardrobes had been replaced with bleached pine doors and a fresh coat of white paint adorned the newly plastered walls. The room was bright and cheery, with our newly transported from England bed in pride of place thanks to Spiros' volunteers. All the room needed was Marigold's homely touch. I reflected Spiros was right: the new bathroom and modernised bedroom would ensure our comfort whilst work continued on the rest of the house.

Seemingly revived, Barry finally put in an appearance, reminding me no provision had been made for his sleeping arrangements and he may be reduced to following Spiros uncle's example and bedding down in the kitchen. Barry was carrying a set of rather grubby plastic chairs

I'd never seen before in my life. "I thought these would be handy for the roof terrace," he beamed.

"I think Barry has just recycled some old rubbish from the bins," Spiros laughed, slapping my brother-in-law on the back in approval.

Too tired to venture out after our travels, we spent the evening relaxing in the surreptitiously scavenged plastic chairs, enjoying the cool mountain breeze and discussing our plans for the future. It was during the course of that evening that Barry first suggested that I should pen a book about up-sticking to Greece.

Chapter 10

Avrio, Methavrio

Once we'd arrived in Meli there were many things we needed to tick off our bucket list of things to sort out as a matter of urgency. Marigold's priority was installing her dream kitchen and mine was purchasing a new car. We needed to visit the bank to check that our transfer of cash from England had arrived in the account, pay Spiros the outstanding balance, and sign some more legal papers to establish definitive ownership of the house. With everything appearing urgent Spiros attempted to introduce us to the Greek concept of *siga -siga*, translated as slowly-slowly. Spiros believed this laid-back approach could be applied to almost everything in life, with the exception of getting his hands on the balance of cash for the house sale; the new hearse needed paying for after all.

It was decided Spiros would drive us into town the next day to sort out the banking and legalities. Vangelis, armed with the requisite measurements, would meet us later at the kitchen showroom. We couldn't do anything about purchasing a car until we acquired residence permits, which would require a visit to the police station.

Still suffering the giddy after effects of travel sickness, compounded by the inevitable vertigo attack he'd suffered whilst sitting on the roof terrace, Barry refused to accompany us to town. Nothing would induce him back on the road until his stomach had settled, and he needed to psyche himself up for the return drive to England.

"I'm happy to stay here and help to get the house in order, it's a big job for Vangelis to tackle on his own and you know how handy I am," Barry offered.

"If you're sure, Barry. Your help would be invaluable; you've such a talent when it comes to DIY," Marigold said, leaving unsaid the amount of times he'd been roped into fixing my own botched attempts at DIY.

"I fully intend to give Vangelis a hand once we've ticked all the necessaries off our bucket list," I said.

Rolling his eyes Barry suggested tactfully, "It would probably be best if you concentrate on the garden. After all I can't just pop round the next time you strike a nail through a water pipe or when one of your crooked shelves collapses. Just remember to buy some decent fans while you're out, I've been sweating something terrible ever since we arrived in Greece, this heat is something else."

"I think there may be the fan in the storage area," Spiros recalled.

"Then I will start by sorting through the stuff in there, at least it will be cooler down below," Barry volunteered.

"Cast your eye over the old furniture and see if there's anything you think could be reclaimed," Marigold encouraged. She silenced me with one of her withering looks before I could voice a sarcastic quip that Barry's less than critical eye had decided grubby plastic chairs retrieved from the bins were a treasured find. Reading my mind she hissed, "At least it meant we had something to sit on last night."

I was adapting well to being driven around in Spiros' air-conditioned hearse, appreciating the consideration afforded to it by other road users. When he didn't have a coffin in the back, Spiros often put his foot down, covering the distance to town in less than ninety minutes. The hearse never got cut off at crossroads or ticketed for double parking. Marigold mocked my tentative suggestion that we invest in a hearse, an idea I immediately binned when Spiros revealed they cost more than the house we'd just purchased.

I was curious about Spiros' repeated use of the word *avrio* meaning tomorrow, ever since he'd assured us we would buy a new kitchen *avrio*, obtain residency permits *avrio*, go to the bank *avrio*, buy a new car *avrio*, transfer the utilities into our name *avrio*, join Greek dancing lessons *avrio*: you get the drift. There were just far too many things to possibly do tomorrow, especially considering the time limitations of operating within a culture where everything closes down at lunchtime.

"*Avrio, methavrio*, there is no rush, relax, appreciate life, enjoy a coffee," Spiros said, taking his hands off the steering wheel in an expansive gesture indicating whenever. "It is how you say a turn of the phrase."

"Like the Spanish concept of *manana*," Marigold noted.

"Exactly, *manana, morgen, avrio*, Greek time, *methavrio*, tomorrow, tomorrow."

"I recognise *morgen* is German for tomorrow, but what is *methavrio*?" I asked.

"The day after tomorrow," Spiros replied.

"*Avrio, methavrio*," I repeated, determined to get to grips with basic Greek.

"All this talk of coffee has given me a thirst," Spiros smiled, slamming the brakes on and double parking outside a coffee shop. Passing pedestrians tipped their heads and made the sign of the cross, making us feel very self-conscious whilst we waited for Spiros to return with three take-out coffees.

Arriving at the bank we were surprised

when the rather unkempt bank manager dressed as casually as usual, surrounded by the ubiquitous haze of cigarette smoke, immediately recognised us, stepping out from behind his corner desk to shake my hand and double kiss Marigold. Unceremoniously booting his current customer from his seat, he gestured for us to sit down; assuring us he was there to help in any way he could. Unfortunately the cash point card he had previously ordered had not yet arrived, but he reminded us it had only been four weeks since it was requested and it would certainly be there *avrio*. By now we understood that although *avrio* meant tomorrow it in no way meant anything would actually happen the next day. He looked rather blank when we suggested the card could be sent to us through the post. Amidst many gesticulations he told us it was impossible and we must call in the bank for the card the next time we were in town, overlooking the inconvenient obstacle of a three-hour round trip on the off-chance it would be there.

With the formalities out of the way, he told us we would need to take a ticket and join the queue for a cashier, to check our funds had arrived and to make a withdrawal of cash. Spiros was ahead of him, having already prised a ticket from the hand of an elderly lady who was fed up of waiting. There were still sixty numbers queued before our purloined ticket so we followed Spiros to the nearest coffee shop to wait our turn, amused when Spiros recalled, "It is just like the Tesco."

Awash with coffee we returned to the bank to await the electronic display of our number. Handing over my passport and passbook I was surprised to almost instantly get my hands on some of the thousands of euros which had arrived in the account that very morning. Within minutes a neat stack of fifty euro notes was whizzed through a modern electronic note counter and shoved into my hands. I was taken aback by the speed of the transaction which contrasted favourably to the painfully slow process of withdrawing a much smaller amount from my building society account back in England. In that instance I had needed to give seven days' notice and then suffer through the teller laboriously counting each note by hand: my casual observation about the amount of germs lurking on bank notes distracted him and I'm certain he deliberately slowed down for the second count.

After obtaining the Greek bank notes I slipped most of them to Spiros to settle the balance of the house payment, before discreetly putting the rest into my money belt. Attaching a clothes peg to the wad of notes, Spiros crammed them into his pocket, seemingly unconcerned about the prospect of muggers.

Our next port of call was a visit to the solicitor to sign on the dotted line. Spiros then gave us the option of heading to the electric or telephone company to put one of the utilities into our name: the other one would need to wait for another day since we had an appointment with Vangelis at the kitchen showroom. We elected to sort out the telephone and internet at OTE, leaving the electricity for another day. Meli had only recently acquired internet cables and although it would prove to be initially slow we were still grateful to have it.

The acquisition of a new kitchen was Marigold's department and she arrived at the kitchen showroom prepared, piling me high with brochures depicting her dream Shaker style kitchen. Although the man in the showroom didn't have anything on display to match Marigold's vision he assured her he could fulfil her remit. Vangelis handed over his sketches and measurements to the kitchen guy who promised to arrive in exactly one week's time to install a classic Shaker kitchen with granite worktops, a ceramic Butler sink and retro-latches. The quote was so cheap in comparison to the prices in the brochures that Marigold had brought over from England that I encouraged her to select a top of the range cooker. In the meantime we could eat in the local taverna and make do with simple fare such as bread, cheese and olives.

Delighted to have achieved so much on our first visit to town we celebrated by treating Spiros and Vangelis to yet more compulsory coffee and the habitual cheese pies. Spiros confided he had a funeral the following day so we must wait until *methavrio* to tackle the next items on the bucket list.

Chapter 11

Vinegar and Honey

Back at the house Barry appeared much revived. He had unearthed two large free standing floor fans in a desperate state of decrepitude from Spiros uncle's storage; with a bit of judicious rewiring and a generous measure of duct tape he had restored them to full working order. This was just as well; it had completely slipped our minds to shop for new ones. Beneath their cooling breeze Barry was hard at work removing the nasty fake chipboard covering the walls of the smallest bedroom.

"I thought you could use this room as your office Victor, you'll need a quiet room to pen your masterpiece," Barry said cheerily, sipping from a glass of translucent red wine.

"Oh, wine, just what I need," Marigold said, grabbing his glass and taking a thirsty gulp.

"Well actually…" Barry started to say, only to be interrupted by Marigold screeching as though she'd inadvertently knocked back a glass of vinegar, "Don't tell me that's the local wine, it's beyond vile."

"No, it's not the local vino, it's red wine vinegar," Barry continued.. "I'd have warned you if you hadn't been so impulsive. I got chatting to a few of the local ladies and they swore blind that a glass of vinegar mixed with a spoonful of local honey is the best remedy for travel sickness. I have to say it's certainly worked wonders on my lingering nausea."

"It's excellent that there's a traditional remedy, and what wonderful news to hear that some of the local ladies speak English, it will make things much easier until we get to grips with the lingo," I sighed in relief.

"Oh no, they didn't speak a word of English, but I didn't let that deter me." Barry said flatly. "You know me, I can get on with anyone, it's just a matter of communication."

"How on earth did they manage to tell you about a travel sickness remedy if they didn't speak English? Don't tell me you've secretly been learning Greek?" I spluttered.

"I popped out to the village shop and the old dears saw I was looking a bit green. It wasn't too difficult to mime nausea, and they picked up on the connection to driving through a bit of charades. Anyway their vinegar and honey remedy is working a treat; I just hope it does the trick when I'm actually driving."

"You must have an iron constitution to stomach that horrid concoction," Marigold commented.

"I'm developing quite a taste for it actually," Barry said, finishing the contents of the glass with relish.

That evening we decided to venture to the village taverna for dinner, thinking it would be an excellent opportunity to introduce ourselves to the locals. Having decided to keep our belongings boxed up until work on the house was finished; we struggled to find some of the items we needed immediately. With no clue which box the mosquito repellent was packed in I was forced to resort to rubbing my exposed areas with Marmite, and with no ready access to my new English-Greek dictionary I pocketed the rather archaic phrase book gifted by Benjamin. Fortunately we'd transported our clothes in suitcases and unpacked them into the new wardrobes, and were thus able to dress up in our Sunday best.

It was still light as we strolled along to the taverna. We appeared to be the objects of curious interest, scrutinised with fixated stares by elderly ladies watering their doorstep pots of basil and by elderly gents, some of whom I recognised as the welcome muscle who'd helped carry our belongings.

"I think you two may be a bit overdressed. Everyone else seems to be much more casual," Barry observed, eyeing my tie and Marigold's high heels. Barry hadn't bothered to dress up, simply changing his sweat soaked tee-shirt for a clean one.

"We want to make a good impression," Marigold said, clinging to my arm and attempting to keep her balance in inappropriate heels. "Ah, here's the taverna, remind me again Victor, what's the word for good evening?"

"It doesn't look like you'll need it," I replied, disappointed to discover the taverna door was locked. "It isn't open."

"It must be, Spiros said it opens every night," Marigold said, despite the clear evidence it was patently closed. "Try rattling the door."

My futile attempts to gain entrance to the obviously closed taverna attracted the attention of an elderly woman in the opposite house. Leaning on a stick, she hobbled slowly to the street, giving me the chance to whip out my phrase book and thumb through the pages in the hope of finding the necessary words to ask why the taverna was closed. The fast paced Greek words she directed towards Barry were punctuated with expressive waves of her walking stick and some unfathomable hand gestures. Marigold and I looked on, completely baffled by Barry's seeming ability to interpret her meaning, floored when he announced, "Litsa says it doesn't open until nine, no one eats at this hour. Oh wait, I may have that wrong, it might not actually start serving food until ten."

"We are far too famished to wait until ten o'clock," I said, checking my watch and noting it was only seven. We'd been up at the crack of dawn to meet Spiros, with only a snack of cheese pies to keep us going.

"Perhaps we can get some cheese and olives from the village shop and enjoy a picnic of sorts on the roof terrace," Barry suggested.

"Won't eating up there bring on one of your turns?" Marigold asked in concern.

"I should be all right if I get another bottle of vinegar," Barry said, determined not to let his vertigo get the best of him.

"The village shop it is then. We'll give the taverna a shot some other evening," I said, thinking we must sort a car out urgently since we had no workable kitchen and the only village taverna didn't start serving food until our bed time.

During our absence in town Barry had found a serviceable table in the storage area and carried it up to the roof terrace to join the scavenged plastic chairs. A set of Christmas tree lights he'd discovered offered the promise of romantic lighting when the sun went down. Settling down to our improvised meal of crusty bread served with juicy ripe tomatoes, cheese and olives, and a plastic bottle of local red, our disappointment at missing out on the taverna disappeared and we appreciated the simple fare in magnificent surroundings. Tiny bats flitted across the sky in the fading light and we were serenaded by the mesmerising sound of cicadas chirping in the distance.

Chapter 12

Fifty Feral Cats

Marigold should have heeded my warning about the sheer insanity of purchasing two pet cats to import to Greece. Our two new additions proved superfluous to requirements on our arrival in Greece; Meli was indeed overrun with a clowder of its own. Our English interlopers soon attracted the attention of every Tom in the area, making it quite impossible to sleep through the literal caterwauling of fifty feral cats on the doorstep.

One particular persistent 'purrvert' took a great fancy to our imported mollies, shocking us with its sheer audacity by staging a pre-dawn break-in through the open balcony doors. Marigold sleepily dispatched me to chase the intrepid interloper out with a broom, a scraggy grey Tom with a distinctive black stripe running sideways across its mutant face. Having seen off the ugly intruder I returned to the bedroom, only to discover Catastrophe and Clawsome had taken refuge from the trilling mating calls of their ardent suitor under our duvet, leaving cat hairs and muddy paw prints all over the bed. The prospect of slipping in beside the cat nappers wasn't too inviting so I decided to take advantage of my rude awakening by tackling the grease coated two ring hotplate. After preparing a paste from baking soda and leaving it to soak into the grease splattered hotplate, I unpacked the electric kettle, a frying pan and some china, and made coffee.

With the hotplate suitably scrubbed, I showered and dressed, slipping out to the village store to purchase the ingredients for a crafty fry-up whilst Marigold slept. By the time

BUCKET TO GREECE

I returned my wife was up and about, fussing over the thought of the starving cats that had disturbed our sleep. Despite their lack of suitable pedigree, Marigold decided to take pity on the feline waifs and strays, pocketing my credit card and making off to the village store for emergency cat supplies. My relief when she returned empty handed, complaining the store only accepts cash, was short lived. Before I could protest Marigold descended on the full English breakfast I had just prepared, cutting it into bite sized pieces and placing it on the doorstep on our best china. I made a mental note not to eat off the willow pattern plates for the foreseeable since goodness only knew what stray germs those ferals were harbouring.

"Feeding the ferals will only encourage them. You can see full well that Catastrophe and Clawsome are in no mood to be aggressively wooed," I pointed out. "If you keep this up the next thing you know we'll be knee deep in kittens and you'll get an unwanted reputation as a mad old cat lady."

"Dig out their travel baskets Victor, I think a visit to the veterinarian is in order," Marigold demanded.

"Well I wasn't exactly implying you should have them put down," I protested, having grown quite fond of the creatures even if unwilling to admit it.

"Don't be so obtuse Victor; we will simply have them seen to. Your point about kittens is one I had overlooked," Marigold said. "Best dig out the phrase book too; I imagine your attempts to sign language sterilisation could give totally the wrong impression."

"And just how are we supposed to transport them to the vets without a car?" I asked.

I could see the cogs turning in Marigold's mind when she realised our lack of transport scuppered her plan.

"We must keep them away from the ferals," she wailed, hastily snatching my breakfast back from the doorstep and shooing the stray cats away determinedly. "I wonder if Spiros will object to the cats riding along in the hearse tomorrow. I suppose we are rather stuck, with no kitchen and no transport."

"We are really reliant on Spiros' good nature until we can sort out our own wheels, unless Barry fancies driving us there in the removal van," I suggested.

"I think Barry has done quite enough driving in his condition. He won't want to do the three hour round trip up to town; those bends could un-do all the good he's derived from that vile vinegar concoction he's been downing. Don't forget he's still got to get all the way back to England," Marigold protested.

"Back to England, are you trying to get rid of me already? I'm in no rush to do that drive yet, the staff can manage without me for another week," Barry said as he joined us. "Is that a fry up I can smell Victor? I wouldn't say no to a full English."

Fortunately, Marigold's imported cats were pampered domestics who showed no interest in venturing outdoors to put themselves at risk of being ravaged by the local Toms. Marigold immediately went on the offensive, determined to keep the local felines away until we could get ours spayed. She apprised Vangelis of the problem when he arrived and luckily he was able to suggest an effective Greek cat deterrent in the form of vinegar. Marigold immediately raided Barry's vinegar supply, liberally spraying it around the balcony doors and all other means of access, in addition to the external stone stairs leading up the front door. Vangelis approved of this measure, noting it would help to kill off the weeds sprouting between the cracks in the steps. The thick coating of moss and green algae lurking beneath the tangle of weeds threatened to turn into green slime at the first sign of rain, a slippery health hazard that I assessed must be tackled at the first opportunity.

With no means of leaving the village, unless feet counted, the three of us decided to muck in and help Vangelis make the house more habitable. Vangelis tasked Barry with restoring the living room tiles to their original glory, a painstaking task that involved scrubbing them with vinegar. It seemed there was no end to the myriad Greek uses for vinegar and I contemplated making an investment in a reputable supplier. Marigold and I were dispatched outdoors to make the stone stairs compliant with health and safety regulations. We were happy to lend our labour since it would help to keep costs down.

Slathering ourselves in high factor sun screen and arming ourselves with likely looking implements from Spiros' dead uncle's tool collection, we joined forces to rid the stone steps of anything invasive. Marigold improvised a knee protector to ease the discomfort of kneeling on the steps to prise the weeds out with the head of a screwdriver, by making use of the bright green shag-pile bathmat previously used as a rug. My mission was to scrape away the moss and green algae with a pallet knife, before dousing the stones with diluted white vinegar and scrubbing them with a hard bristled brush.

The task proved quite arduous due to the heat of the sun; it was slow going since we needed to constantly wipe droplets of perspiration from our sweaty brows. Our efforts were rewarded when inch by inch the stones were restored to weed and moss free zones, creating a pleasant approach to the entrance. As the sun beat down and butterflies flitted, Marigold was distracted by the scuttling sounds emanating from the overgrown garden; convinced snakes were lurking in the undergrowth.

Joining us outdoors for one of his many frappe and cigarette breaks, Vangelis confirmed Marigold's worst fears that snakes could well be slithering through the weeds. Luckily his ready solution to the problem was to surround the perimeter of the house with Greek mothballs as a snake deterrent, sending Marigold dashing off to the village shop to purchase *nafthalini*.

"Fancy that, a solution that doesn't involve vinegar," I quipped.

After praising the progress we'd made on the stairs, Vangelis and I stood in companionable silence, contemplating the enormity of the task involved in reclaiming the garden.

"It is big job, Victor. It's a pity I can't help you out when the inside is finished but another building job is lined up."

"It needs a bulldozer running through it," I sighed, overwhelmed by the jungle growth.

"Or I could just borrow you a goat, it cost much less," he offered.

"Lend me," I automatically corrected, adding, "But what a stroke of genius, I'd be happy to borrow a goat if you have one to spare."

"No, I not have goats Victor, but I can borrow one to eat its way through your garden. I think I can borrow one very cheap."

"I think you mean hire one," I corrected, explaining borrowing tended to be free.

"What on earth is that vile stench?" Marigold demanded, returning from the shop and glaring disdainfully at Vangelis' cigarette. Her accusatory stare seemed misplaced when we were suddenly inexplicably engulfed in billowing clouds of noxious smoke.

"It smells like burning plastic," I complained.

"That will be Maria up to her usual tricks," Vangelis nodded sagely.

"Maria, the old dear next door?" Marigold queried.

"Oh yes, she has the bad habit of burning plastic, she won't be told," Vangelis confirmed between bouts of coughing triggered by potentially toxic fumes.

"Well we must put a stop to it at once, she must be breaking goodness knows how many health and safety ordinances pertaining to air pollution," I said, attempting to sound confident but actually uncertain what unknown Greek codes our neighbour may be violating.

"I told you, she won't be told," Vangelis coughed. "She's been up to her tricks for years; it drove Spiros' uncle to the ouzo."

"Are you telling us that the bad blood between Spiros' uncle and the sweet old lady next door was down to her?" Marigold spluttered.

Like me, she had jumped to the conclusion that it was Spiros' uncle who must have antagonised his neighbour in some way to provoke their long standing feud, though Marigold's hackles had risen when she'd caught Maria rifling through our box of kitchen spices.

"Well would you be happy living next door to a cantankerous old woman who burn the plastic day after day?" Vangelis asked, stopping short when he realised we did indeed live next door to the budding arsonist. "She refuses to put her rubbish in the bins for anyone to go through and examine, preferring to set fire to it every morning."

"How bizarre," Marigold said. "Is there a proclivity amongst the villagers for rummaging through the bins? And how on earth does she manage to accumulate so much plastic in the first place."

"There are no bin 'rummagers' apart from the odd fox," Vangelis said, whipping out a pencil and paper to add the new word to his expanding list of interesting English vocabulary.

"The wine comes in plastic bottles," I pointed out, wondering if our neighbour was burning the evidence of a secret tippling habit.

"Still, she must be stopped; such practices release dangerous chemicals into the atmosphere that are damaging to the environment."

"Dangerous?" Vangelis questioned.

"Oh yes, you'd better take Victor's word for it, he was an environmental health inspector before he retired," Marigold said proudly.

A look of confusion spread over Vangelis' face as he said, "Spiros tell me Victor got paid to eat in restaurants."

"Spiros has the wrong end of the stick," I insisted, watching Vangelis' confusion grow as he grappled with the idiom.

"You'll need to take Vangelis with you to translate if you intend to have it out with Maria about burning plastic," Marigold advised.

"Keep me out of it," Vangelis cried. "I'm not one to go round making enemies. I don't do the feuds, they are bad for business."

Desperate to avoid any more of the toxic plastic fumes we headed inside, only to be immediately asphyxiated by the potent smell of vinegar emanating from the tiles.

Chapter 13

Puntoed Up

The remainder of our first week in Greece flew by in a flurry of activity, with several more trips up to town in Spiros' hearse. Spiros put his foot down; refusing to play chauffeur to the cats, claiming it would be unseemly if any corpses ended up covered in cat hairs, remarking; "You English have odd habits, so sentimental about cats but not wanting the kittens."

There was summary disappointment when

the kitchen man failed to materialise on the promised day with Marigold's much longed for Shaker kitchen. I asked Vangelis to give him translated short shrift over the telephone when the kitchen man came up with the by now all too common excuse of *methavrio*.

We were delighted when the unkempt bank manager finally handed over our cash point cards, though disappointed to discover they were as yet ineffective as debit cards.

"We work on the technology, *siga-siga*, next year maybe," the bank manager apologised.

"*Avrio chronon*," I agreed, showing off the Greek skills I had acquired from the phrase book.

"*Tou chronou*," the bank manager corrected, earning me one of Marigold's withering looks for my attempt to show off.

Spiros skilfully negotiated the transfer of the electricity and water supplies to our names, a straightforward task involving the handing over of our new tax numbers and photocopies of our passports. Spiros insisted it was pointless to go shopping for a car until we had the residence permits necessary to facilitate a sale, so we stopped in at the police station on one of our trips back from town, the station being located equidistant between town and home. We were sent off with a flea in our ears since the paperwork could not be completed without the inclusion of the passport photos we hadn't realised we needed. It was then that we grasped Greek bureaucracy didn't run quite as smoothly as we'd imagined; we would need Spiros to drive us all the way back to town to acquire the necessary passport photos. There were no handy booths spewing out instant photos behind a curtain when a coin was inserted. Instead we needed to visit a professional photographer who told us to return in two days to collect the developed images.

Finally armed with the necessary photos we paid a return visit to the police station, eagerly anticipating getting out hands on our new Greek residence permits. The officer in charge studied each of the papers we presented pertaining to health insurance, income and residency, giving the impression he was eager to find something remiss he could send us away to correct. He scrutinised the passport photos that made us look like a pair of serial killers, comparing our images to the photographs of what appeared to be Greece's 'Most Wanted' pinned on the notice board behind his desk. Seeming quite miffed that we weren't a pair of criminals he could immediately arrest and interrogate with heinous methods of torture, and that all our paperwork was actually in order, he finally gleefully pronounced that we would need to provide an additional photocopy of our passports. This didn't appear to present a problem as his desk was next to a photocopier machine, but he insisted it was out of paper and we would need to go elsewhere for our copies.

"It is not the good for Greek public servants if everything is the simple," Spiros explained, ushering us into the town hall, or *dimarcheio*, where he knew someone who had access to the photocopier. "If everything was straightforward the people would be out of the job for life."

Returning to the police station we had to wait in line once again since the officer in charge was now on his coffee break. It was hard to tell the difference as his break involved sitting at his desk sipping coffee and enjoying a leisurely cigarette, exactly the same habits he'd indulged in earlier. He appeared quite happy to flout health and safety regulations by lighting up underneath the 'No Smoking' sign. Much later, after watching him slowly type up the paperwork with two fingers, we gushed with gratitude to finally have our hands on the blue permits which would allow us to become car owners. It felt strange to be grateful for having something in our possession which as EU citizens we didn't actually need, but Greek bureaucracy apparently demanded we acquire unnecessary documents to purchase a car. It wasn't even a money making scam since the permits were free, unless one counted the price of professional photographers and photocopy paper.

Our complete reliance on Spiros for transport made Marigold just as enthusiastic as I to get on with purchasing a car. The Shaker kitchen we had ordered was such a bargain price compared to its English equivalent that we had ample funds left over to purchase a brand new car, rather than buying second-hand as we'd originally intended. It made sense to buy new since we had discovered second hand Greek cars were not subject to depreciation and were in fact quite pricey. Spiros, once again roped in as chauffeur and translator, drove us to the Fiat

Punto dealership in town, declaring we couldn't go wrong with a Punto since it was the most popular car in Greece and ten thousand Greeks couldn't possibly be wrong. Marigold initially favoured another model, but the sight of a gleaming red Punto complete with manual sun-roof finally tempted her when the dealer said he had one in stock which we could drive off the forecourt that very day. Neither of us was interested in any car that would need to be placed on order. The kitchen man's failure to put in an appearance after the promised seven days convinced us that any kind of arbitrary timescale was a bit too tenuous for our needs.

Naturally there were reams of paperwork to complete before we could drive away in the Punto. The dealership was on the outskirts of town, but we would need to head into the centre to visit a proscribed bank to pay for a *paravalo*, a paper which would show we had paid the necessary tax to transfer the car to our name. Naturally the bank involved was a different one to our branch of the National Bank of Greece which I would need to visit to withdraw the cash to pay for the Punto, since naturally the dealer preferred to deal in cash. Spiros was happy to go along with the dealer's suggestion that I hop on the back of one of his minion's mopeds to visit the banks as it would be much quicker nipping through traffic on two wheels.

Marigold, alarmed at the prospect of my riding pillion and withdrawing so much cash, calmed down when I agreed to stash the cash in my underpants until I could deliver it back to the dealer. She had adapted said underpants by sewing a zippered pocket just below the waistband, not entirely convinced my money belt was discreet enough to deter the determined muggers she imagined on every street corner. Spiros suggested he and Marigold have coffee and cheese pies whilst they waited, a suggestion Marigold agreed to with alacrity when Spiros assured her she could swap the cheese pie for a *bougatsa*. It was amazing how quickly Marigold had become quite addicted to these tempting creamy custard pies doused in icing sugar, with never a thought to her waistline.

Perched on the back of the moped and clinging onto the middle of the greasy mechanic, I began to understand the Greek propensity for making the sign of the cross. It proved to be a harrowing trip to the centre of town as he weaved dangerously in out of erratic traffic, employing many of the gesticulations favoured by Spiros when the hearse was coffin free. I joined an endless queue at the bank where the *paravalo* needed to be paid, cursing that they hadn't developed such an enlightened practice as the ticket system used by the National Bank and Tesco's cheese counter. After an interminable wait to pay the transfer tax it was back on the moped for another hair raising ride to the National. The unkempt bank manager sprang out from behind his desk to greet me, asking how he could be of service. Unfortunately the services he offered didn't extend to grabbing the cash I needed, so I was forced to take a ticket and wait my turn. When the cash was finally handed over I received some very odd looks when I followed Marigold's instructions and stuffed the notes in my zippered underpants.

Back at the dealership the dealer practically purred with pleasure as he counted the cash, assuring me he would take care of registering the car in my name and sorting out insurance. "He says you can collect your green registration booklet next time you are here," Spiros translated, adding, "You should to drive up for it

very soon, you will have to produce it if the police to stop you or you pay the big fine." It
seemed our days of driving into town weren't
over, but at least I could look forward to doing
it under my own steam in future.

Spiros brushed off our enthusiastic thanks
for all his help with the typical *tipota*, before suggesting we buy him dinner that evening at the
Meli taverna. "You won't get so many the
strange looks if you are with a local your first
time. And don't wear your best dresses, it isn't
your Ritz," he said with a knowing wink.

I assured him we would look forward to
sharing an evening meal in his company at our
local, whilst mentally noting our presence in the
village had indeed attracted some strange looks.
I'd been unable to dispel whatever strange no-
tions the locals had about us, held back from
confronting them due to my inability to communicate the obvious question, "Are my flies
undone or have I sprouted two heads?" Thank-
ing Spiros again for his endless help, we bid him
goodbye, with Spiros laughingly reminding me
to remember to drive on the left.

"I don't think I fancy getting to grips with a
left-hand drive car Victor. It's a bit confusing,"

Marigold said when we drove off the forecourt with a welcoming breeze drifting in through sunroof. There and then I realised I'd been relegated to the role of ferrying her about, a very inconvenient state of affairs as I'd be forced to forgo any alcohol when we went out.

Chapter 14

A Meal Fit for Kings

Mindful of Spiros' advice we made a point of dressing down that evening for our second attempt to visit the local taverna. Even so it took ages for Marigold to get ready since she wanted to make a good impression; when she finally put in an appearance I could tell her casual look was very much studied. My below the knee cargo shorts paired with socks and sandals received one of her withering looks; she told me they looked quite ridiculous with my tie. There was no time to change into something that would win Marigold's approval as Spiros was outside in the hearse, waiting to drive us to the taverna. We considered this an extravagance since we could cover the distance on foot in less than five minutes, not realising it was a typically Greek habit to drive everywhere and park as close to the door as possible.

Cynthia, the English lady Spiros was crushing on, unfortunately turned down his invitation to join us. Marigold didn't buy her rather lame excuse that she was washing her hair, whispering to me that, "She must be a bit standoffish, no one pulls out that old excuse since showers and hairdryers were invented. It only worked back in the days of washing one's hair in the sink before curling it in rollers."

"Perhaps she isn't attracted to Spiros and was trying to turn him down gently," I whispered back.

"Still, you'd have thought she'd have made an effort to meet us fellow Brits," Marigold insisted, ignoring my avowed preference to refer to us as Europeans.

"Well we are sure to run into her soon enough,"

V.D. BUCKET

I said. "I expect it's just Spiros she's trying to avoid, dating an undertaker isn't everyone's cup of tea; it's a bit of a dead end."

It was a relief to find the taverna door propped open with a large tin of olive oil, rather than locked, though the establishment was empty. Bare tables and uncomfortable looking hard backed chairs filled the space, with the kitchen set off to one side at the back. The only light in the room came from the windows overlooking the street; the fast fading light was just enough to illuminate the dancing dustballs disturbed by the light breeze blowing in through the open door, making me grateful I'd had the foresight not to venture out sockless in my sandals. A seemingly antique cast iron wood burner, or *somba*, attached to ancient black pipes held together with silver duct tape, was obviously responsible for the blackened ceiling festooned with soot stained cobwebs.

Leading us to an empty table littered with out of date newspapers, Spiros bellowed out "Niko." Taking our seats, Marigold, Barry and I surveyed the premises in disbelief. My first impression was that it would fail a health inspec-

122

tion miserably and I made a mental note to keep well away from the bathroom facilities. Fortunately the kitchen area was open to view, allowing me to keep a beady eye out for any dubious practices.

"It's a bit spit and sawdust," Barry observed, an understatement if ever I'd heard one. I could tell at a glance that it wasn't Marigold's type of place since it lacked any kind of atmosphere, but knew she would put up with it to watch me squirm. For some unfathomable reason it amused her to witness me forced to compromise on my exacting hygiene standards: she knew I wouldn't embarrass Spiros by criticising his local in his presence.

"It is the simple place but it have the everything you need, good food, good wine," Spiros assured us, adding with an expansive wave of his arms that encompassed the whole room, "and good company."

Marigold couldn't resist pointing out the obvious. "But we're the only ones here."

"People will come when Nikos fires the grill," Spiros said. "We come early, I know you British like to eat in the afternoon."

"We're Europeans," I corrected.

"And it has gone eight o'clock," Barry pointed out.

"That still afternoon in Greek time," Spiros laughed, before once again yelling "Niko." When his deafening yell elicited no response Spiros headed outside, saying, "I go look for him."

"It's a bit of a dump," I hissed once Spiros was out of earshot. "We could be taking our lives in our hands by eating anything prepared in that primeval kitchen."

"It's certainly not the welcoming village taverna I imagined, it rather lacks ambiance," Marigold conceded. "We must make the most of it tonight, we can't offend Spiros, but at least we can venture further afield in future now that we've got the Punto."

As the designated driver I groaned inwardly at her words, wondering if the taverna might be more appealing after a good mopping out. Perhaps I could drop a subtle hint about lax hygiene standards when the owner put in an appearance and shame him into dusting away the cobwebs.

Spiros returned, beaming broadly. "Nikos come now, he was picking the tomatoes. He grow everything he serve, he make the wine, he make the olive oil, he make the cheese, he kill the animals for the grill. He has the joke that only the water is nothing to do with him."

"That must keep him busy," Barry said.

"Too much work when you think the Nikos and his wife Dina are in their late seventies and have no help, their son Kostis is useless, always off hunting or chasing the women," Spiros sighed.

Our chat was interrupted by the arrival of a giant of a man, clear blue eyes twinkling in his weatherworn face, only a thick growth of stubble marring his handsome features. Clutching a plastic crate brimming with ripe tomatoes emitting the juiciest aroma, he approached our table, saying "*Fresco domatoes, to kalutero, nai.*"

I nodded enthusiastically in response to his words, amazed by my ability to make sense of them, recognising *kalutero* was the best and *nai* was yes. Adam's assurance that many English words derived from Greek ones was verified by my recognition that fresh tomatoes demonstrated a fine example of learned borrowings.

Spiros' introduction to Nikos flummoxed me somewhat since he had told us the owner was in his late seventies, but this vigorous man enthusing over his fresh tomatoes exuded youthful energy and didn't look a day over sixty.

"Welcome, welcome to Meli my friends," Nikos warmly declared in hesitant English, crushing my hand in his larger one. "It is good to have, how you say, fresh body in village."

"Fresh blood," I automatically corrected. The idiom obviously confused Nikos. He dropped his tomatoes on our table and dashed off into the kitchen, returning with a first aid kit before Spiros could clarify the language mix-up. When it became clear there was no fresh blood spill requiring an urgent need for plasters or bandages Nikos burst into the obviously well practiced spiel he saved for foreigners.

"Everything here is freshest, no supermarket *scoopeethia*, how you say, the rubbish. I grow all my food and kill my animals for grill. I make my olive oil and wine, only the water nothing to do with me." Nikos said proudly.

"I can't wait to see your menu," Marigold said, giggling politely at Nikos' water quip even though she had already laughed when she first heard it from Spiros.

"No menu, whatever I kill I grill. You want food now? I go get Dina, she still in field. Later I play bouzouki, you will like," Nikos said, filling four tall water glasses with rose wine from a one and a half litre plastic bottle. *Spitico mou, to kalutero.*"

With that he flicked some switches in the back of the kitchen, flooding the whole room with buzzing fluorescent yellow light before leaving the taverna unattended, speeding off up the road on his moped, defiantly helmetless. The yellow light cast sudden shadows on the suspended cobwebs clogged with dead mosquitoes. I revaluated my opinion that the cobwebs should go; having neglected to smear marmite on my exposed extremities I considered it preferable the mosquitoes flew into the spider trap rather than feast on my blood.

"*Yamas,*" Spiros toasted as the four of us clinked glasses of homemade wine. My glass appeared clean enough so I risked a sip of its potent smelling contents, taken aback by the delicious flavourful richness that immediately transported me to a sun dappled vineyard.

"This is absolutely sublime," Marigold enthused.

"It's certainly got a kick to it," Barry approved.

"*To kalutero,*" Spiros boasted before adding, "the best," just in case we needed a translation.

I considered my initial impression of the taverna had perhaps been too hasty as Nikos' homemade wine was far superior to anything we'd tasted elsewhere. Nikos himself seemed to be a larger than life character I would enjoy getting to know. The taverna had appeared soulless until Nikos put in an appearance, but his expansive personality immediately breathed life into the dusty neglected space and I imagined he had some intriguing tales to tell.

In no time at all Nikos returned, his wife precariously balanced side-saddle on the moped. Dina, her tiny stature dwarfed by her husband's towering presence, warmly welcomed us in Greek. Her sparkling eyes were almost lost in the crease of her smile, her now faded beauty reflected in her pleasant features. A few stray wisps of grey hair peeked from her black headscarf; she straightened her drab brown dress neatly over her trim figure before tying a voluminous orange apron in place.

Nikos disappeared outside through a side

door to fire the grill and Dina scurried into the kitchen, returning almost immediately to present us with a huge basket of bread and a half-full bottle of olive oil. The bread and oil was quickly followed by a plate of cheese doused in yet more olive oil and garnished with fragrant oregano. It was accompanied by a huge bowl of salad comprising generous chunks of the freshly picked tomatoes, crisp slices of red onions and green peppers, all dotted with fat black olives and drenched in yet more olive oil. It was so mouth-wateringly delectable that I abandoned all my scruples about kitchen cleanliness and tucked in with relish. Barry, a life-long avoider of salad being more of a chips and pie man, appeared to be a sudden convert, extolling the freshness of the food and comparing the sweetness of the tomatoes to strawberries.

Dina's arrival signified the taverna was open for business; gradually some of the local men began to drift in, taking their seats and giving us the once over with suspicious stares. Most of the clientele appeared to be comprised of hardy pensioners, seemingly the default age group of the village. My hand was repeatedly crushed as Spiros finally made formal introductions. Marigold was spared the ordeal of suffering repeated kisses from strangers, Spiros explaining she would have to make do with nods of greeting until she was formally introduced to the spouses of the village men. It appeared the local habit was for the men to head to the taverna alone, their womenfolk apparently preferring the comforts of their clean homes.

Throughout the course of the evening only one Greek woman other than Dina put in a fleeting appearance. It was the elderly lady, Litsa, who lived in the house opposite the taverna whom we had met briefly when she'd hobbled down to gesticulate the opening hours. Hoisting herself up the step into the taverna with the aid of her walking stick, she shuffled over to one of the elderly gents, discreetly sneaking a small tinfoil wrapped package onto his lap as though she was making a delivery of illicit drugs. Spotting Barry sitting nearby, her wrinkled face burst into a smile and she made a beeline for him. Barry jumped up to greet her, forcing her to reach up to cluck his cheek fondly. Dismissing Spiros' attempts to introduce us with a curt wave of her hand, she hobbled off.

Intrigued to discover if her discreet delivery

contained suspect white powder or something more innocuous, I stared in fascination as the elderly gent unfurled the package to reveal a bulb of raw garlic. Taking a pocket knife from his trouser pocket he gave it a quick wipe on the tail of his shirt before skilfully slicing the garlic into tiny slivers and piling them on top of his oil drizzled bread. Fifteen minutes later the old woman returned to the taverna clutching a carrier bag. Hobbling over to Barry she dove into the depths of the bag, pressing a plastic bottle of vinegar and a glass jar of honey into his hands. Spiros translated, saying. "Barry, she make to you the gift of this homemade vinegar and honey to cure the curse of your travel vomit."

She beamed with pleasure when Barry leant down to her diminutive height to plant a tender kiss of thanks on her gnarled cheek.

"Word of your unfortunate condition has spread through the village," Spiros explained to Barry as the old lady hobbled back off into the night, a definite spring to her step as she swung the now empty carrier bag, her black clad figure immediately enveloped by the darkness outside.

"It's a pity she isn't thirty years younger,

she seems to have taken quite a shine to my brother," Marigold whispered. She would like nothing more than for Barry to discover love in Meli so he might be tempted to hang around. Being very fond of her brother, she would feel the distance between them keenly, once he returned to England.

"I hope you don't make the old fellow jealous," I said to Barry, nodding towards the old chap engrossed in eating raw garlic.

"No problem, he is the brother of the widow Litsa, not the husband. The field is free for the Barry to, how you say, court her," Spiros laughed.

The side door opened and Nikos appeared, engulfed in a cloud of thick smoke wafting indoors from the grill. He was balancing several platters heaped high with lamb chops which he distributed between the tables, calling out for Dina to hurry up with the potatoes. His wife carried a piping hot plate piled high with home-made chips fashioned from home grown potatoes, seasoned with sea salt personally gathered and prepared by Nikos.

"These are the best chips I have ever tasted," Barry said earnestly, causing Dina to blush with pleasure when his fine praise was translated by Spiros. The meat was tender and tasty, so succulent I was sure it had been gambolling around in the fields that very morning before Nikos earmarked it for the grill.

We nodded our eager agreement when Nikos asked us, "Good *nai*, good food, the fresh?" before pulling out a chair to join us. The atmosphere in the taverna was now completely transformed, everyone enjoying the splendid food and the excellent wine in convivial company. Following my introduction to an elderly gent called Panos, I attempted a conversation with him that seemed to focus on fruit. I hoped I hadn't inadvertently offended him in some way with my ignorance of local customs when he abruptly departed the taverna without bidding goodbye, and I noticed, without paying,

As Marigold chased the last olive round her plate Nikos invited us to step outside to view the wood fired bread oven where Dina made the wonderful loaves she sold to the villagers. We were so impressed we placed an immediate order for her regular Friday bread. Nikos pointed out an area used for outdoor dining in the height of summer, now empty apart from a cat curled up comfortably on one of the plastic chairs and a collection of impressive basil plants sprouting from old olive tins. I breathed in deeply, appreciating the fragrant scent of basil permeating the air.

"Come, now I play bouzouki," Nikos invited, ushering us back indoors. Strumming his instrument he crooned a classic Greek song in a deep melodious voice. As we listened, transfixed by the music, Panos returned, pressing a plastic carrier bag full of luscious green grapes into my hands, freshly plucked from his very own vine. It was a relief to realise he hadn't been driven away by any inadvertently offensive behaviour on my part, but rather motivated by a spontaneous gesture of generosity. The grapes proved so delicious I was inspired to suggest we establish a trellis on the roof terrace.

As the evening drew to a close, we agreed we were lucky to have such a fabulous local taverna. I decided I would not allow a few cobwebs and dustballs to detract from the truly wonderful experience we'd enjoyed. If we hadn't already decided to become regulars by the time Nikos scrawled the bill on the paper tablecloth, we would have been won over by the ridiculous price of such an excellent night out.

"There must be some mistake, this can't be right, seventeen euros for dinner for the four of us," I said to Nikos, calculating the favourable exchange rate made it less than a tenner in English pounds.

Drawing himself up to his full height Nikos assured me wasn't trying to rip me off and the price was indeed seventeen euros. Brushing the bread basket aside he scribbled some more on the tablecloth, whilst itemising the prices: "Meat for four, twelve euro, bread one euro, cheese one euro, salad one euro, potatoes one euro, wine one euro, everything seventeen. The music no charge."

"But it's so incredibly cheap," I spluttered, adding for clarity, "little money," desperately trying to assure Nikos I thought he had under, rather than overcharged us. Seventeen euros would only cover the cost of the lamb chops for two people down on the coast, never mind all the extras we'd indulged in.

"No supermarket *scoopeethia* price, my lamb, my wine, my oil, my cheese, my salad, my bread," Nikos said, his voice getting steadily louder as he reeled off each item before winking broadly and adding, "Little money, you not drink the expensive water or Fanta."

Our protracted departure involved bidding goodnight to the locals in our still very limited rudimentary Greek. Nikos crushed our hands again and Dina ventured out of the kitchen to deposit kisses. Assuring them we would return again very soon we finally left, with Marigold hissing, "At those prices we can afford to eat out every night if I don't fancy cooking."

I sighed in relief at her words, knowing I would be able to enjoy a tipple of Nikos' *spitico* without having to worry about driving home. Despite the rather grubby surroundings, we had dined on a meal fit for kings created from the freshest of ingredients, and to top it all off the price was a pittance.

Declining Spiros' offer of a ride home in the hearse, we enjoyed a pleasant stroll home in the moonlight, relaxed and merry, happily ignoring the strong smell of fried chips that clung to our clothes.

Chapter 15

An Awful Ex-Pat Encounter

I t was obvious the cats could sense something amiss when we attempted to round them up for their trip to the vet; the sight of their travel baskets enough to send them frantically scurrying into hiding. I could only imagine their reaction if they knew what plans we had in store for their internal plumbing. Eventually after resorting to lacing their food with sedatives we successfully caged them, escaping with only minor scratches.

We were just loading the baskets into the back of the Punto when the kitchen man arrived unannounced, scuppering our spaying plans. Marigold's excitement at the prospect of her dream Shaker kitchen being installed was palpable. The kitchen man began by fitting the new top of the range cooker into its allotted space, before unveiling the dented monstrosity of a stainless steel sink he was about to plumb in. Marigold went into an immediate meltdown, screaming, "That isn't the ceramic Butler sink I ordered."

Baffled by her histrionics the kitchen man looked to Vangelis to translate.

"He say he could not to find the Butler so he bring you this nice shiny one, only a bit used."

I noticed it looked suspiciously similar to the old one that Vangelis had ripped out and dumped at the tip.

"Tell him it won't do, I have my heart set on a Butler," Marigold screeched.

"He not understand; he say sink is sink," Vangelis translated.

Leafing through one of her kitchen magazines, Marigold thrust a picture of a Butler sink under the kitchen man's nose, demanding, "Can he spot the difference now, the style, the colour, the material is all wrong."

Scratching his head the kitchen man appeared to concede there was indeed a subtle difference between a second hand dented stainless steel sink and a brand new ceramic Butler.

"He say he work round it. He fit the kitchen units and take the sink you not want away. He say the sink you want impossible, yes impossible."

"Well it's very inconvenient," Marigold said, her anger draining away at the prospect of the bespoke Shaker being installed, even if it would remain temporarily sinkless.

I had to physically hold her back to prevent her from attacking the kitchen man when he finally revealed the nasty cheap plywood he had nailed together into the most basic cabinet doors. Vangelis struggled to keep up translating Marigold's complaints as she pointed out the obvious, stating, "There is nothing remotely Shaker like about these doors, the style is all wrong, there are no distinctive inset grooved panels, these are just plain and nasty. They have been cobbled together from inferior materials, I expected alabaster stained maple. He promised me alabaster maple."

"I can paint," the kitchen man protested, ducking to avoid the empty tin of cat food Marigold hurled in his direction. Vangelis reminded him he had indeed promised nothing less than maple and he couldn't expect us to be foisted off with a kitchen that bore no resemblance to the design we had ordered.

Fortunately Marigold clearly had an ally in Vangelis. He understood she had set her heart on a certain style of kitchen and the inferior crap the kitchen man was trying to pass off would never pass muster. Following a heated discussion the kitchen man presented an invoice for the new top of the range cooker, reluctantly loading the stainless steel sink and the imitation kitchen back into his van, all the while muttering Greek expletives under his breath.

"Please don't translate," I begged Vangelis. Certain the kitchen man was maligning my wife; I hoped to spare her blushes.

"He's really landed us in it," Marigold snapped. "What are we going to do now? We've wasted ten days waiting for him to turn up with that nasty excuse for a kitchen. Perhaps Vangelis knows where we can find a

Shaker one in town."

"We can't afford a genuine Shaker kitchen," I pointed out, clocking the preposterous prices in the brochure. "We spent the money we saved on ordering what we thought was a bargain price Shaker on purchasing the new Punto."

"I not see anything like this quality in town, maybe you find in Athens," Vangelis said apologetically, flicking through the Shaker brochure.

"I should have realised it was too good to be true, expecting my dream kitchen for less than the price of one from IKEA," Marigold sighed.

"I have the much experience fitting the IKEA kitchen, I do in the many foreign houses," Vangelis suggested.

"I'd rather go that way than risk another botched kitchen," Marigold said pragmatically. "Vangeli, if we choose an IKEA kitchen do you think you could find me a Butler sink?"

"Of course, you may not get the kitchen you dream of but I find you the sink, I make for you the impossible to happen," Vangelis agreed, patting her shoulder supportively. "I know what it is when a woman set her heart on something, Athena was exact the same about the waterbed; I had to order from the Germany."

"You have a waterbed?" Marigold asked, mouth gaping in amazement.

"We did, but the cats make too many the punctures and the water flood the kitchen. It was no loss, it make me seasick."

"I can imagine," Marigold cooed sympathetically.

"At least you still have a top of the range cooker," I interjected, attempting to dispel the vivid images of Athena and Vangelis flopping round on a waterbed.

"We can't continue to live without a kitchen in the house, it's just not practical. Let's get one from IKEA tomorrow," Marigold said decisively, already resigned to the fact that a Shaker one was out of our price range.

I hadn't spotted the distinctive Swedish superstore during our extensive drives around town with Spiros so I quizzed Vangelis as to how the other foreigners had got hold of their IKEA kitchens. He told us that some ex-pats had shipped the flat packs over with the rest of their belongings, but one couple had driven all the way up to Thessaloniki to purchase one from the new IKEA store.

"It would take weeks to have one shipped over from England," Marigold said.

"Is the store in Thessaloniki the nearest one?" I asked Vangelis.

"It is the only one in Greece," he replied.

"Then we must drive up to Thessaloniki, we could turn it into a mini-break Victor," Marigold said, overcome with sudden excitement. "We can book into a luxury hotel, do some sightseeing and check out the shops."

"And what about the cats, we can't just leave them to their own devices, they haven't mastered the tin-opener yet," I argued, hoping to let Marigold down gently. I had no intention of frittering away cash on unnecessary mini-breaks involving luxurious hotel stays and shopping sprees, so soon into our Greek sojourn.

"I suppose we could ask Maria to pop in and feed them," Marigold hesitantly suggested.

"There is one fly in your vinegar," Vangelis interrupted. "You will not to be able to fit the new kitchen into the Punto. Better if I drive you there in my van and check the measurement of the kitchen, you pay the petrol. We be there and back in one day, it only nine hour each way if I put the foot down. No need to throw the good money on hotel and no have Maria in rummaging through your boxes. Rummaging, I very much like that word."

Genuinely touched by Vangelis' kind offer to spend upwards of eighteen hours at the wheel, I thanked him profusely, his gesture going above and beyond his building remit.

"*Tipota,*" Vangelis responded, before taking his phone outdoors to make calls about the sink.

"It is very kind of Vangelis to drive us all that way," Marigold said, already resigned to the loss of her imagined mini-break.

Several cigarettes and phone calls later Vangelis re-joined us with excellent news.

"Good news, I find the dream Butler in shop in town," Vangelis said. "And tomorrow is the last day of the IKEA sale; you can get the twenty of the percent off. We set off at the four in the morning and I fit it *methavrio.*"

"Cooee," a loud female voice trilled from the doorway. "I hope you don't think we're being nosey but there appears to be a basket of cats getting a bit frantic in that Fiat Punto parked outside and we thought they might be something to do with you."

BUCKET TO GREECE

Drat. With all the kitchen commotion consuming the best part of the morning we had completely neglected the cats, still sedated and caged in the car. Barely glancing at the couple blocking the doorway who'd alerted me to my forgetfulness, I pushed them aside and dashed downstairs. I discovered the Punto surrounded by every stray Tom in the area, caterwauling their ardent desire to ravish our tabbies who had been woken from their drugged stupor by the unwanted attentions of their posse of ardent suitors. Demonstrating the nimble agility of a cat burglar, the persistent purrvert I had previously ejected with a broom had managed to sneak in through the car window I'd left slightly ajar, sending our pair into a state of hissing panic as it pressed its whiskers against their basket and sank its claws into the car's brand new leather upholstery. There was no mistaking the scraggy grey stray with its distinctive black stripe running sideways across its mutant face.

Dumping the disagreeable looking potential rapist on the pavement I grabbed the cat baskets, whisking a traumatised Clawsome and Catastrophe to safety. By the time I returned to the house Marigold was deep in conversation with the couple I'd barely glanced at in my haste to rescue the cats.

"This is Harold and Joan, they live here in Meli," Marigold said in introduction.

I noticed they appeared a mismatched pair; the stout woman with a brassy dyed blonde hairdo standing a head taller than her equally rotund but diminutive mate. Far too much of their peeling red skin was revealed by their bizarre choice of outfits; he sported nothing but a pair of indecent budgie smugglers beneath a Hawaiian shirt, conveniently open to best display the paunch I suspected from his beery breath was a beer-belly. Her bat wings wobbled like jelly when she adjusted the sheer black wrap presumably meant to cover the flab she had managed to pour into a bikini. I surmised they were a couple of sun worshippers, presumably blissfully ignorant of the dangers of over cooking their bodies and seemingly oblivious that their attire was not only age inappropriate but most definitely unsuitable for dropping in unannounced on their new neighbours.

Marigold continued, "Harold and Joan have a little house on the other side of the village square."

"It's actually much larger than it looks, and it has a swimming pool, the best pool for miles," Harold insisted, obviously trying to impress us before adding in an accusatory tone, "We've been by to say hello more than a few times but we never seem to catch you in, you always appear to be off out gadding."

"We've had a lot of business to attend to in town, getting everything official in order," I explained, wondering how Barry had managed to avoid them if they'd been persistent callers.

"Rather you than us, it's a complete nightmare trying to get anything done in this darn country," Harold opined, a look of open derision plastered on his face as though he was stuck in some third-world hell-hole.

"A complete nightmare," Joan parroted. "It's unbelievable how few of them bother to learn English; it makes everything so much more difficult."

"Well we are in Greece, surely it is up to us to make the effort," I argued, my hackles rising at her contemptuous tone.

"How long have you lived here?" Marigold asked in what I recognised as feigned interest, knowing her well enough to spot the signs that she hadn't taken to them.

"It's been almost three years now," Harold practically spat. "It's really bad form no one told us you were in the market for a house, we're desperate to sell up and move back to England. I'm sure our place would have suited you far better than this old dump. Typical of the Greeks to not bother mentioning we were after a buyer."

"We happen to like this property, it suits us, and as you can see we are in the process of modernising it," I defended.

"Well don't expect them to make a proper job of it," Harold openly sneered. About to rigorously defend Vangelis' professionalism, I noticed he was nowhere to be seen and immediately leapt to the conclusion he had made himself scarce, having no doubt crossed paths with this obnoxious pair on earlier occasions. Still, my curiosity was piqued as to why they were so desperate to move back to England after making such an adventurous move in the first place. They spared me the bother of asking by launching into a litany of gripes.

"It's a pity you didn't meet us before buying, we would have told you straight what a mistake you were making. How many times have I said we should have rented before buying?" Harold said.

"Every day," Joan assured him. "Every day you say if only we'd rented we could have been back in old Blighty by now."

"That's what I say. Course it was the wife who was so insistent on moving here in the first place. Phhh, women, what do they know?"

"You thought it was a good investment," Joan meekly countered, obviously well used to her husband's public put downs.

Ignoring her comment Harold continued, "Well you've made a mistake buying this place, no doubt about it. Come winter you'll really regret it. There's nothing to do in this godforsaken village, not even a decent pub, not that there's anyone worth drinking with, the Brits are all stuck-up snobs and the Greeks don't bother to learn English."

"It wouldn't have been so bad if we'd bought on the coast, in the summer there's plenty of tourists to have a drink with," Joan interrupted her husband.

"Well that was all right when we first got

here, but we can't even do that anymore since the police got me for drink driving," Harold moaned.

"Oh, that was terrible, we'd had a nice day on the beach with a few bevvies and then the police stopped us. I had to spend the night in a hotel because they locked Harold up until the next day. They wouldn't let him out until he paid an enormous fine."

"Outrageous it was, I told them I was British," Harold said, bloated with righteous indignation.

"He did, I'm British he said," Joan repeated. "Of course they don't have any time for Brits out here unless they're after our money."

Her words washed over me, not worthy of a reply. Our experience to date was that the Greeks we had met had been warm and welcoming. I considered how Spiros had gone above and beyond any obligation he may have felt as the seller of our house, chauffeuring us round in his hearse, freely giving hours of his time as we conducted business unrelated to the purchase. I considered how readily Vangelis had volunteered himself for the eighteen hour drive to Thessaloniki in a gesture of true friendship, and I recalled how Panos had pressed his grapes on me so generously.

"So now we're really stuck up here in the sticks," Joan's voice interrupted my reflections. "It isn't fair to expect Harold not to enjoy a drink, and it's risky for him driving back after a few with the police waiting to pounce. And the state of this village, if it's not the water that's off then it's the electricity."

Allowing his wife time to breathe Harold chipped in with his two cents worth, complaining, "Their telly is dreadful, we tried to watch it but it's all in Greek and if they do show an American film it's ruined by the infernal adverts that go on forever."

"We can't get Eastenders or Emmerdale, that satellite dish Harold paid a fortune for doesn't work properly, Harold said wiring it up right was too much for the Greeks," Joan lamented.

Mention of the monstrous satellite dish that marred the horizon helped identify the house this couple lived in. It was the one that had been stripped of all typical Greek character, the quaint wooden shutters replaced with great big windows that must make the place a veritable hell-hole of heat in summer.

"Then of course the village shop simply doesn't cater for British tastes, Harold's tried telling them they need to start selling proper British food."

"Not that they take a blind bit of notice, how many times have I told them we have to have our Yorkshire teabags, black treacle and marmite? Can you believe they make some vile tea out of twigs?" Harold snorted.

"I think you'll find that is *tsai tou vounou*, a mountain herb," I corrected, wondering if the offer of a jar of marmite and a packet of Tetley teabags might be enough of a bribe to get rid of the gruesome twosome.

A look of confusion spread over their reddened faces as they said in dismayed unison, "Oh, you speak Greek."

I immediately surmised they hadn't bothered to learn a single word of the local lingo in their three year stay if they were impressed by my knowing the Greek word for tea.

"*Nai ligo, matheno,*" I replied, certain they would be clueless I'd told them 'a little', and 'I am learning.' The look of bafflement etched on their faces showed they hadn't even bothered mastering the most basic vocabulary of their new homeland. Joan had to go and make herself look even more stupid by piping up in a mis-guided attempt to impress us, "We know how to order beer in Greek, don't we Harold?"

"Indeed, two *beera*," he boasted whilst winking, blatantly dropping a none-too-subtle hint that they wouldn't be averse to the offer of a drink. I knew from my cursory study of the Greek phrase book that the plural of *beera* was *beeres*, but I had no intention of prolonging this unwanted encounter by correcting him or of breaking into the supply of Amstel I kept on hand so Vangelis could enjoy a hard earned drink at the end of his daily labours.

"It was so nice of you to drop by," Marigold lied through her teeth, "but I'm afraid we do need to be getting on."

Completely ignoring my wife's polite hint that they needed to leave, Harold continued, "You must come and use our pool, we couldn't stand it here without our pool, and of course this old place doesn't have one."

"Yes, you must," Joan chimed in. "Shall we say tomorrow at noon? Harold can fire up the barbecue."

"I'm afraid that's out of the question, we have important business to attend to in Thessaloniki," I said loftily, having no intention of revealing our important business involved a trolley dash round IKEA before their sale ended.

"Oh, well we must definitely do it when you get back," Joan insisted desperately, visibly deflated by the lost opportunity to show off their pool.

"That we must," Harold boomed, a bewildered expression on his face when we didn't immediately jump at his offer.

"Well we really do have things we must be doing," I said, forcefully steering Harold towards the door.

"Don't forget, we must get together for that barbecue by our pool as soon as you get back from Thessaloniki. Us Brits have to stick together and put up a united front against these foreigners," Harold shouted over his shoulder as they headed downstairs.

Marigold and I clung onto one another in amusement, stifling our laughter when the sound of Harold's continued carping carried up the stairs and we overheard him say, "Well really, they weren't very sociable, you'd think they'd have at least offered us a drink."

"**W**here have you two been hiding?" I asked when Barry and Vangelis finally reappeared.

"We hide in your office when we hear the Harold and Joan arrive," Vangelis said.

"I don't blame you, they were perfectly ghastly," Marigold chortled.

"We've had to employ quite a lot of avoidance tactics, they're very persistent," Barry said. "Luckily Vangelis warned me about them the first time they turned up uninvited so I just pretended I didn't speak English to get rid of them. In my work clothes they mistook me for a labourer so I was spared the pool invitation."

"Ingenious, I wish we'd thought of that," I said. "Vangeli, I don't like the way they so freely snuck up the stairs. Do you think you could erect a gate downstairs?"

"I think you need it Victor, otherwise the Harold and Joan will be popping in to, how you say, borrow the cup of sugar every day."

"More likely a cup of *beera*," I laughed, inwardly worried that we could end up wasting a lot of time avoiding them. "A pleasant evening in the local taverna would be ruined if they turned up and gate crashed our table."

"Not to the worry," Vangelis reassured me, "Nikos banned the Harold and Joan when they complained the place was filthy and the wine tasted as though he'd stomped on the grapes with the smelly feet."

Chapter 16

Die for You

Being a habitually early riser I had no problem with the pre-dawn start to our road trip to Thessaloniki. Marigold, never a morning person, was not inclined to be sociable at such an early hour. Hoping to detract attention away from her uncommunicative state, I attempted to engage Vangelis in general chatter until he turned up the volume of his radio, informing me he preferred to sing along to the music rather than talk whilst driving. There-

after the only respite from his tuneless rendi-
tions of the greatest Greek chart toppers was offered when he double-parked the van to stop for
takeaway coffee. By the time we reached Thessaloniki I was word perfect in the lyrics of 'Die
for You', the 2001 Greek entry that had placed
third in the Eurovision, apparently still so popular the radio station felt the need to blast it out
twice every hour.

The familiarity of the forced route march
through each furniture section of IKEA made us
temporarily feel as though we were back in
Manchester, only the Greek signs dispelling our
feeling of deja vu. After assuring Marigold that
the kitchen she selected would be, dimension
wise, a perfect fit, Vangelis beseeched her help
in locating an English style potato masher as a
gift for Athena. When he'd seen the one we had
brought over with us he'd marvelled at its prac-
ticality, extolling the design of what we considered a common kitchen implement, as a triumph. Learning they were not readily available
in Greece, Marigold added an extra one to our
trolley in case we should have the misfortune to
run into any potato mashing emergencies.

Always suspicious of the ingredients in

mass produced hot-dogs I steered my companions past the in-store cafe and helped Vangelis to load our new flat packed kitchen into the back of the van. Vangelis scoffed at our suggestion of finding a restaurant for lunch, instead producing a packed lunch of homemade *spanakopita* prepared by Athena which we duly ate in the car park whilst sipping on take-out frappes. As we munched our way through Athena's delicious spinach pie Vangelis fed us titillating snippets of local gossip. Following our encounter with 'the' Harold and Joan, Vangelis reassured us that we wouldn't need to avoid the fellow Brits we were yet to meet, since they were on the whole perfectly pleasant types. My dislike for the couple we'd met the day before grew exponentially when Vangelis told us that Harold had employed him to do some work on the patio wall surrounding the swimming pool, only to subsequently stiff him over the bill.

Vangelis also confided that Cynthia, the English woman who Spiros was crushing over, had apparently caught Barry's eye. Needless to say this was the first we'd heard of it and Marigold lost no time at all in interrogating Vangelis, hoping to prise every last morsel of information from him. He wasn't very forthcoming, simply stating, "They meet in the shop, Barry be how you say infatuate, but worry to step on the toes of Spiros."

"We must invite her over for drinks on the roof terrace," Marigold declared, obviously wanting to check out Cynthia to see if she was a suitable match for her brother. She was eager to see Barry re-marry; he'd been single ever since a messy divorce a decade earlier. These days Barry was not so much a confirmed bachelor, just wary of women, having given up on dating following an unfortunate experience.

Responding to a Lonely Hearts ad in the Manchester Evening News he'd met up with a woman for a blind date. Although he sensed she was sending out creepy vibes he politely stuck out the evening, resisting the temptation to leg it through the bathroom window as ungentle-manly. During their brief encounter she demon-strated deplorable table manners, greedily wolf-ing a bar snack of scampi and chips washed down with a double Campari and orange, all the while getting too familiar with Barry's thigh, convincing him she had him earmarked as the dessert course.

BUCKET TO GREECE

Following their dire date she turned into a besotted stalker he could not shake, harassing Barry endlessly with love letters penned in purple ink and persistent phone calls that led to him being forced to go ex-directory. In the end he was obliged to seek legal advice and obtain a restraining order when she took to loitering at the end of his street, announcing to all his neighbours that they were engaged.

Being very fond of her only brother, Marigold had been dreading the day of Barry's already delayed departure from Greece. He had stayed on for longer than he'd originally intended, in part to help with the work needed on the house and in part to delay the inevitable onset of travel sickness that the long drive back would trigger. The removal company he owned was now booked solid with removals and needed him and the van back; he was due to leave us *methavrio*, having promised to spend his final day helping Vangelis to screw the new kitchen together.

"It will be too late today by the time we get back to invite her over for drinks, and tomorrow is Barry's last day," I pointed out.

Marigold sighed in frustration, recognising

that even if Vangelis didn't stop for constant coffees he still wouldn't have us back in the village much before midnight.

"I will have to think of a way to facilitate a meeting between them tomorrow," she pondered, the scheming cogs of her brain visible to my naked eye. If she could manage to set Barry up with the elusive English woman, he may be inclined to fly over regularly to visit, particularly if the local Greek remedy for travel sickness proved effective on planes.

There was no time to spare for sightseeing on the long drive back, a journey only punctuated by Vangelis' repeated breaks to grab yet more take-out coffees. In need of the toilet facilities, I accompanied Vangelis into one cafe. Joining him in the queue I didn't realise I was tapping my feet and singing along to the lyrics of 'Die for You' when it came over the radio until I felt the unsettling stares of the other patrons. Thinking they would never see me again I decided to ham up my performance in a re-enactment of the dole queue scene in the 'Full Monty', earning me a round of applause from my audience and fine words of praise from Vangelis: "*Bravo*

Victor, you are not after all, how you say, the stuffy."

Chapter 17

The Albanian in the Garden Shed

Considering the lateness of the hour when we returned from Thessaloniki, Vangelis had warned me he would put in a late appearance the next morning and not to expect him before ten, leaving Barry and I to make a start on the kitchen. Marigold claimed she needed a lie in as the persistent racket of her husband and builder tunelessly warbling along to 'Die for You' had left her with a shocker of a headache.

Since it was his last day Barry was eager to get an early start on the kitchen. Flatly stating it was a two man job, he initially gave me the benefit of the doubt, graciously allowing me to start removing the yet to be assembled cabinets from their boxes. His frustration soon mounted when I insisted we should logically follow the indecipherable IKEA instructions to the letter by identifying all the components and screws before starting.

"Frankly Victor you are just a hindrance, the instructions aren't there to be followed as you'd well know if you didn't always botch up anything practical."

Reluctant to let him work on alone since he was technically a guest, I busied myself with collecting the superfluous packaging.

"Do you need this little doodah or should I sling it out with the rubbish?" I asked, noticing something metal glinting amidst the packaging.

"That's a hinge Victor; just put it down before you lose it. If you want to do something useful pop downstairs and see if there's a drill in the storage."

"I thought that…"

My words were cut short by Barry telling

me to clear out; he couldn't concentrate on visualising the wall plan with me chuntering in his ear. Reluctantly leaving him to it I headed downstairs where I immediately spotted a suspicious figure making its way furtively through the jungle of overgrowth masquerading as the garden.

"Halt," I cried, using the cardboard box I was holding as a defensive weapon, unable to identify the intruder in the early morning darkness. As the figure continued to approach I gripped the cardboard tightly, contemplating disabling whatever it was by sticking the box over its head. I realised I may have overreacted when the figure morphed into that of a man, one hand extended in greeting. The man was of short stature, slight and dishevelled, giving the appearance he'd slept in his shabby clothes. I was immediately struck by his youth; guessing him to be about thirty-years old I considered that would make him the youngest person I'd thus far encountered in the village.

"Guzim," he said in a strong guttural accent.

"Guzim," I replied, presuming he was greeting me in his native tongue, most likely some East European language I guessed.

"*Ego Guzim,*" he said, thumping his chest to indicate his name was Guzim. Pointing towards the stone shed off to one side of the garden he added, "*Meno to micro spiti.*" Struggling to decipher his accent it suddenly occurred to me he was saying he lived in the small house. Small or otherwise, the use of the word 'house' to describe the battered stone shed which I quite coveted for garden storage struck me as gross hyperbole. Mirroring his movements I thumped my own chest, a spontaneous move I immediate regretted when my rib cage groaned in pain, before pointing at the house behind me and saying, "*Ego Victor, to spiti mou.*"

There followed a hearty handshake between us. Before taking his leave Guzim attempted to press a dusty cap into my hands, saying "*Seeka, yia sena.*" His meaning became clear when he grabbed my cardboard box, tipping the contents of his dusty headgear inside. Peering into the box I saw about two dozen plump purple figs leaking rich red juices into the cardboard, only understanding he intended I should take them when he repeated "*Yia sena. Yamas.*"

Embarrassed to have no handy fruit on my person that I could offer him in return, I gesticulated for him to wait one minute whilst I dashed up the stairs to retrieve one of the bottles of Amstel I kept in for Vangelis, speculating that Guzim's use of the word *Yamas* meant a beer wouldn't go amiss even though it wasn't yet eight in the morning. The beer was received with an almost toothless smile; the shabby shed dweller risking the few remaining teeth in his mouth by using them to prise the bottle top free. With a hearty swig of breakfast beer and a dismissive nod he sidled towards the road, striding across the pathway running adjacent to my stairs.

I waited until later in the day when Vangelis broke off from the laborious task of assembling the kitchen to slip outside for a crafty cigarette, before raising the subject of Guzim.

"He is Albanian, he do the casual labour, he say he send the money back to the wife in Albania. He just back in Greece from a visit to the wife," Vangelis said, explaining why I hadn't happened to notice anyone living in my garden until this morning.

"He told me he lives in that stone shed, but

it barely looks habitable," I observed. After meeting Guzim I had taken a closer look at the shed, shocked to discover a camping stove left dangerously close to the bedding when I attempted to peer through the window. It appeared to be a simple one room structure, not at all suitable for habitation since it seemed to lack any bathroom facilities.

"Yes, he work many hours to buy from Pedros."

"Pedros?"

"The dead uncle of Spiros. He take money from the Guzim even though I think illegal."

"So the sale may not have been legal?" I asked, only to be met with a typical Greek shrug.

The stone shed stood off to one corner at the bottom of the garden. I had noticed that the only access was either over the garden wall or through our garden, necessitating passing by our exterior stairs to the road, access which would be blocked once Vangelis fitted a lockable gate to deter Harold and Joan from turning up uninvited. It struck me as a strange set up and one which hadn't been alluded to in the legal papers.

"I suppose we must give Guzim a key to the gate then when you fit it," I reluctantly suggested, still mulling over his strange living arrangements.

Raising an eyebrow, Vangelis stubbed out his cigarette, before heading wordlessly back indoors. Following him inside I noticed that work which had been progressing well on the kitchen had now come to a grinding halt, Marigold's appearance having distracted Barry as she quizzed him relentlessly about his interest in Cynthia. Vangelis reddened, realising he was responsible for the loose lipped gossip pertaining to Barry's romantic interest in the English woman.

"It's nothing sis, I only met her the once and I leave tomorrow," Barry protested.

"I could invite her over for drinks on the roof terrace this evening," Marigold persisted.

"And make yourself look as desperate as Harold and Joan trawling for new friends," Barry sighed, hoping his put down would be enough to make Marigold drop the subject.

"I'm only thinking of you Barry; it would be good for you to meet a new lady friend, nothing would make me happier than seeing you settled with a wife."

"Just let it drop, you're jumping the gun trying to marry me off to a woman I only exchanged a few words with in the village shop. If I don't get on we'll never get this kitchen finished before I leave. It's a two man job and Victor won't be of any use to Vangelis if it isn't sorted before I leave," Barry pleaded in exasperation.

Although tempted to take offence at this slight, I knew Barry spoke with no malice since it was patently true I struggled to fathom one end of a screwdriver from the other and all my attempts at DIY ended in disaster. Instead I invited Marigold to join me on the small balcony overlooking the street to discuss the matter of the Albanian living in the stone shed.

Somewhat taken aback to discover someone actually lived in the shed in our garden Marigold said, "Whoever heard of such a thing as beds in sheds?"

"I can only surmise the planning regulations must be very lax over here, his living arrangements would certainly violate numerous health and safety, not to mention fire regulations, back in the UK," I said.

"You said it was just one room, so where on

earth does he do his ablutions?" Marigold asked.

"Considering the rather ripe smell he emitted I expect his ablutions are confined to a quick wash down under the outside hosepipe, weather permitting," I replied, recalling the hosepipe I'd seen coiled up by the door of the shed.

"But Victor, our guest bedroom overlooks the garden. This just won't do, imagine if we have guests and they are confronted with the sight of a naked man washing his bits under a hosepipe? I'm not at all happy about the thought of a strange man living in our garden shed," Marigold said, her brow furrowed in nervous anxiety.

"Well according to Vangelis it isn't technically our shed as Spiros' uncle sold it to Guzim," I told her.

"But it's in our garden," she cried in confusion.

"I plan to speak to Spiros about it; no mention was made of the matter when we signed the papers and our plan to fix a lockable gate is going to create an access issue. Vangelis indicated the sale may have been illegal," I said, "Or could he have meant that Guzim is here illegally? In his defence he appears to be perfectly harmless, not to mention generous, he insisted on plying me with free figs."

"Nevertheless you must speak with Spiros at the earliest opportunity," Marigold advised. "I'm not sure I like the idea of a possibly illegal Albanian bedding down in our garden shed and flashing his bits under a hosepipe."

"I will," I promised, equally unnerved the more I thought about the strange set up.

Determined to have the last word Marigold demanded, "Make sure you do," before waltzing off to retrieve Barry's laundry from the washing machine in the bathroom to peg out on the garden line.

Chapter 18

Spiros Lands on His Fundament

Alone on the balcony my attention was caught by an attractive woman with glossy brunette hair. She was duct-taping a poster to the lamp post in the street below. My curiosity was piqued as I pondered if it perhaps advertised some local festivity. About to head down to investigate, I noticed Spiros cycling along the street, his preferred mode of transport being a bicycle for village business that didn't necessitate the hearse. Swivelling his head sideways, his full attention fixated on the attractive woman rather than the road ahead, he failed to spot the pot-hole beneath the balcony, directly in his path. The impact of the front wheel sinking into the concrete crater sent the bicycle sprawling, sending Spiros flying over the handlebars. Concerned he may he be hurt, since naturally he flouted all health and safety advice by refusing to wear a cycling helmet, I dashed down to proffer assistance.

"I'm fine, I'm fine, just how you say, the little tumble," Spiros insisted, wiping blood from a nasty looking gash on his forehead. "Luckily, the Cynthia not witness the indignity of my fall."

Looking around I was surprised to see no sign of the woman who'd been sticking the poster to the lamp-post; surely she couldn't have failed to see Spiros so comically come a cropper. Physically restraining Spiros to prevent him getting up until I could check out his injuries, I hollered upstairs for Barry to bring down the first aid kit whilst Spiros launched into a tirade of Greek expletives, cursing the pot-hole he blamed for his fall.

"Well if you'd had your eye on the road instead of ogling that attractive brunette you'd have seen the pot-hole," I pointed out.

"It is true I was distracted by the Cynthia's beauty," Spiros sheepishly admitted shamefacedly, realising I'd witnessed the whole sorry escapade.

"Well she certainly demonstrated a callous lack of compassion in taking off so quickly without bothering to stop and offer assistance," I remarked, dismissing Cynthia as a heartless floozy not worthy of Barry or Spiros' interest.

"She have the back turned and how you say, the Walkman, in her head. I am happy the Cynthia not see, is not good for my reputation to land on my fundament," Spiros declared, amazing me with his choice of out-dated formal English vocabulary.

"Better than landing on your arse mate," Barry crudely piped up, arriving with the first aid kit. "Ooh that looks nasty. Better let Victor take a look while I see if I can knock your front wheel back into shape."

"I'm fine, I'm fine, stop to the fuss," Spiros protested, attempting to rise but falling back languidly as though he was the consumptive heroine in a nineteenth century melodrama.

"You need urgent medical attention, you may well have suffered concussion," I told him, sticking a vibrant blue plaster on his forehead to hold the gaping gash together until a medical professional could assess how many stiches he needed.

"What's going on," Marigold enquired, late to arrive to the scene of the accident and closely followed by Vangelis.

"Spiros came off his bicycle," I said, sparing his blushes by neglecting to mention Cynthia's possibly unwitting part in the calamity.

"That blue plaster looks ridiculous; don't we have any flesh coloured ones?" Marigold asked, obviously more concerned with aesthetics than possible concussion. I had deliberately made a point of stocking the first aid kit with brightly coloured plasters since flesh coloured ones could easily be dislodged from fingers and end up in food preparation, presenting a choking hazard if they remained undetected.

"Help me get him in the Punto," I said to Barry, quizzing Vangelis for directions to the nearest hospital.

"Take him to the doctor in the next village. You can't miss it, it have the bright red cross outside," Vangelis advised, urging me to hurry before we all choked on the noxious fumes suddenly wafting down to the street from Maria's garden. She had clearly made a late start on her dangerous daily routine of burning plastic.

"I'll come along for moral support," Marigold offered.

Fortunately Spiros was declared concussion free. His forehead gash required seven stiches which he pragmatically decided would give him a dashing air. No doubt all references to bicycles and pot-holes would be omitted when he embellished the tale of how he acquired his rakish scar. I noticed with interest that he bartered the doctor's fee, paying for the doctor's proficient skill with a needle with the promise of a tin of olive oil. I considered this to be a very practical way of going about things and determined to barter my invaluable advice on the most effective health and safety measures to implement to secure the most sterile environment, were I ever to require medical attention. It seemed inappropriate to raise the subject of the Albanian living in the stone shed in my garden whilst Spiros was being stitched up, but I resolved to have it out with him at the first available opportunity.

Marigold and I returned home, confident speedy progress would have been made installing the kitchen in our absence. Whilst Marigold went to check if the washing was dry, I lingered on the street, eager to see what the poster Cynthia had stuck on the lamp-post was all about. I was taken aback to come face to face with a glossy photograph of a missing cat. The features confronting me were none other than those of the shabby grey Tom with a distinctive black stripe across its mutant face, the feline menace intent on raping our tabbies which I had presumed was a feral stray. I found it hard to imagine this depraved and predatory creature was someone's beloved lost pet.

My perusal of the poster was disturbed by hysterical screams emanating from the garden. Recognising Marigold's piercing cries I worried that Guzim may have surprised my wife by returning to take a midday hosepipe shower. I dashed to her side, only to discoverer her attempting to batter a goat with a pair of Barry's jeans.

"This vile creature got into the garden somehow, I found it eating the washing," Marigold cried, desperately trying to shoo the goat away. Her attempts were futile; the goat stood its ground, contorting its head and twitching its mouth to get a good grasp on the denim leg, turning Barry's jeans into the contested object in a violent tug-of-war. Relieved that my wife had been spared the traumatic shock of being flashed by a naked Albanian, I immediately jumped to the conclusion that the intrusive goat had something to do with Guzim. It seemed far too much of a coincidence that on the very same day Guzim appeared in my garden, a random goat should roll up and decide to eat the washing. Fortunately it hadn't gnawed its way through any of mine of Marigold's clothes since she had only put Barry's things through the wash in preparation for his departure.

Marigold's screams brought Barry and Vangelis running. My assumption that Guzim was somehow responsible for the goat was immediately dispelled when Vangelis declared, "I borrow you the goat for the garden Victor." Recalling the discussion we'd had about Vangelis possibly borrowing a goat to tackle the overgrowth I realised he'd gone ahead without bothering to alert us to its presence. Taking charge of the situation Vangelis tethered the goat with a rope secured well away from the washing line, leaving it to chomp its way through the weeds without inflicting any further damage on Barry's now much depleted wardrobe.

Chapter 19

Almost Perfectly Normal

Vangelis and Barry were joined in the kitchen by Eduardo, an electrician who turned up to sort out the wiring on the integrated spotlights. Eduardo, another Albanian, was not Vangelis' first pick of tradesmen; he lamented the area was desperately short of good Greek electricians since they could earn more money in the cities. Vangelis' comment of, "Fingers crossed he not, how you say, make the bodge job this time," in no way reassured me that Eduardo was the man for the task. I could see Marigold's blood pressure reaching near explosion point when Eduardo hopped onto the new granite worktop without bothering to remove his boots, so I gently steered her into the bedroom and suggested she take a siesta.

"But it is Barry's last day," she said.

"Well he won't thank either of us for getting in his way. If we leave them to it the kitchen should be finished before evening."

It was actually late afternoon when Vangelis proudly announced the new kitchen had been successfully fitted, complete with integrated spotlights wired up by Eduardo. Vangelis had ripped down the plastic sheeting that separated the kitchen area from the living area and removed the dust sheets that had concealed most of the room. The grand salon in its entirety was revealed to us for the first time since our initial viewing of the house. The transformation was quite remarkable, barely resembling the cluttered space once filled with Spiros' uncle's old tat.

The newly fitted kitchen took pride of the

place to the left of the room, a kitchen island marking a clear division between the living space. Light flooded in through the newly painted balcony doors, creating a focal point in the centre of the room, and the floor was a masterpiece of beautifully restored ceramic tiles. The rich colour of the exposed brickwork on the fireplace wall added immeasurable character to the room and the traditional fireplace promised warmth on cold winter evenings. The remaining walls gleamed with a fresh coat of white paint on newly laid plaster, and the chandeliers boasted a full complement of light bulbs.

"You can finally get hands on Victor, by giving us a hand to lug the furniture up out of the storage area," Barry announced. "Have you decided what you want to put where?"

"I think I can safely say Marigold will have the last word on furniture placement," I said, deferring to my wife's superior taste in home decor. She had never doubted that this room could be transformed into the centrepiece of our home and I was happy to stand back and let her direct the three of us as we struggled to lug two imported cream sofas up the stairs, followed by a dining room table and six chairs. Marigold's placement of a stunning ornamental mirror over the fireplace made the grand salon appear even larger in the reflected light.

"Vangeli, you have done such a wonderful job," Marigold gushed in appreciation. "The kitchen may not be a Shaker, but it looks marvellous."

"And tomorrow I collect the housemaid to go in the kitchen," Vangelis said.

"Hold on old chap, we never said anything about employing domestics," I protested.

"I think Vangelis means the Butler, rather a housemaid," Marigold laughed, realising he had muddled up his sinks and servants.

"Forgive me, I never hear of the Butler until Marigold set her heart on it," Vangelis clarified. "Tomorrow I fit the sink, I need then two, maybe three more days to tile the kitchen, it is hard to calculate the time exact; I get used to the Barry's help. Then I can crack on and finish the rest of the house."

"Don't worry, I have a bucket list of everything that needs doing," I reassured him. In truth the bulk of the modernisation had been done. We had a new bathroom, kitchen, salon and bedroom. Work only remained on the spare bedroom, office and entrance hall, and cosmetic work on the roof terrace. The goat had already made a sterling start on the garden though I reflected unless it was particularly avaricious we'd still be better off going with the bulldozer option.

"I'm happy I had the time to come out to lend a hand," Barry said. "I expect Vangelis may have been driven to strangling Victor if he'd got involved with the re-fit."

"What is this you say?" Vangelis protested. "I like the Victor very much, or course I not make the murder."

"You say that Vangeli, but you haven't experienced his attempts to help with odd jobs. He's not, as we say, very handy," Barry explained.

"I just feel guilty that you've spent all your time here working Barry, you've not even had chance to leave the village," Marigold commiserated.

"That was down to the lingering effects of the travel sickness. Anyway I saw plenty of Greece on the drive down from Patras and I've enjoyed my strolls round the village, it is totally charming."

"Well you must promise me you'll come back soon for a proper holiday," Marigold pressed. "We can swim at the coast and explore some old ruins."

"That all depends if the local remedy for travel sickness works. You know how I am about flying, not to mention it's a long drive over from the airport in Athens, especially if I'm already queasy from the plane," Barry said realistically.

"We're all keeping our fingers crossed that the vinegar and honey remedy does the trick once you're actually in motion," I assured him.

"Now that this room is finished we need to plan a shopping trip to town," Marigold said in a steely voice that welcomed no argument, busying herself strategically placing a collection of ornamental scented candles around the room. "We need some turquoise cushions for a splash of colour, some tasteful vases and some typically Greek paintings to add the finishing touch."

"We can combine your shopping trip with our visit to the veterinarian," I said. My suggestion could not have been made at a more apt moment as the sudden incursion of the grey

Tom with the mutant face, into the salon via the open balcony doors, reminded me we really did need to get Clawsome and Catastrophe spayed before they were ravished.

"First it's a goat in the garden and now that ugly Tom in our living room," Marigold complained, looking round for a broom to chase the brazen interloper away before it could pounce on the new kitchen wiring it was giving the evil eye.

"Hold on a sec," I advised, suddenly recalling the Tom wasn't actually a stray but Cynthia's beloved missing pet. "That cat belongs to Cynthia, she plastered a poster up outside saying it was missing."

"You didn't tell me you'd met her," Marigold accused.

"I haven't," I replied. "I saw a woman sticking a poster on to the lamp post and Spiros mentioned it was Cynthia."

"Make a grab for it Victor and don't let go," Marigold instructed, the visible cogs of her brain going into overdrive. "I'll fetch one of the cat's baskets and Barry can take the foul creature back to its owner."

It was almost midnight before Barry put in a smiling reappearance after returning Cynthia's vile cat, a twinkle in his eye and a definite spring in his step. Completely disregarding his earlier statements expressing his reluctance to visit due to the onerous travel involved, Barry announced he'd try to fly out again the next month.

"Don't even think about attempting to put up Marigold's bookshelves Victor, I'll do them when I get back."

"You've changed your tune," Marigold said in delight. "I suppose that's something to do with your new lady friend."

"Don't go on at him Marigold, you can see he's blushing," I said. "You got the cat back all right then Barry?"

"Yes indeed. Cynthia says she'll pop by soon to make your acquaintance. She's been a bit wary of new Brits ever since Harold and Joan roped her into one of their pool partied, but I told her she has nothing to fear from you two and that you're almost perfectly normal."

Chapter 20

A Dark Start to the Day

Sleep had been an elusive hope, almost within my grasp until the Chinese water torture began, the persistent drip-drip of water rousing me sometime before dawn. Creeping quietly to the bathroom to avoid disturbing Marigold, my socks and the hem of my pyjama legs immediately turned soggy when I stepped into a wet patch in the hallway. Surmising it must be raining in through the ceiling below the roof terrace I made a mental note to ask

Vangelis to deal with it as a matter of urgency. After wringing the excess water from my socks I felt the icy chill of the tiles penetrating my now bare feet, reminding me I must delve into the still unpacked boxes heaped in the ground floor storage space. The sudden abrupt change in weather made it far too uncivilised to contemplate another day without slippers.

The torrential rain that had prevented me from sleeping finally stopped. I mosied into the new kitchen, planning to watch the sunrise with a warming shot of much needed caffeine whilst preparing a flask of vinegar and local honey for Barry to take on his travels, hopefully countering any nausea on his return drive to England. My plan was thwarted when the kettle failed to fire into action. Immediately jumping to the conclusion the incompetent electrician Eduardo had bungled the wiring, I groped round in the dark feeling for a torch, hoping to shine some light on the fuse box in the hallway, cleverly disguised behind a rather gaudy reproduction of an icon depicting our Lady of the Sign, Platytera. In this instance it appeared Eduardo was blameless since the fuses all stood to attention.

V.D. BUCKET

Peering through the kitchen window revealed nothing but darkness. There were no friendly lights twinkling in nearby houses and I pondered if this was down to the early hour or one of the frequent black out's Harold and Joan had ranted about.

I was disturbed from my reverie by a sudden sharp knock on the front door, surprised that anyone would decide to call at such an inappropriate hour. Thinking up a ready excuse in case it was Harold getting in super early to try to pin us down for a pool party, I opened the door cautiously. Wielding my flash light as a weapon, just in case the early caller had nefarious intentions, I temporarily blinded the figure lurking in the darkness before relief washed over me when I discovered the caller was Guzim rather than Harold.

Greeting me with his almost toothless smile Guzim proffered another cap full of figs, a generous gesture I repaid with another bottle of Amstel. After twisting the bottle top off with his teeth Guzim stood awkwardly on the doorstep, raising the bottle of beer and saying "*Yamas*': surely he didn't expect me to join him in a beer swigging breakfast. Fortunately I had memorised the Greek for 'you are from Albania' to use as an ice-breaker in the eventuality of running into my shed dwelling neighbour again. "*Nai, nai, apo Alvania*," he confirmed before breaking into fast paced Greek I struggled to understand. Finally identifying the Greek word for England in his monologue I interrupted to say, "*nai, eime apo Anglia.*"

This obviously convinced Guzim that I could actually make sense of his words, so I threw "*siga-siga*" in his direction in an effort to slow him down. Obligingly, Guzim proceeded to speak with slow deliberation and careful enunciation, though with my very limited vocabulary this didn't actually help much at all. Before swigging the last remnants of beer and taking his leave, I simply nodded along as he told me he had thirteen children in Albania, or it could have been three. For all I knew he could actually be childless and regaling me with tales of his thirteen, or three, chickens. Perhaps it was wives since Albania was a Muslim country, but Vangelis had only mentioned the one. The indecipherable encounter convinced me that as soon as work on the house was complete the first order of business must be Greek lessons.

The power was conveniently restored just in time to cook Barry a full English. Since it was Barry's last morning Marigold prised herself out of bed early. Completely oblivious to the atrocious weather we had suffered or the hours endured without light, she immediately launched into a complaint about me lighting all her best scented candles so wastefully. Barry mentioned that he didn't have much to pack since the borrowed goat had eaten its way through most of his wardrobe, but Marigold dismissed his complaint, saying "Cynthia won't be impressed with your usual style. Look on the bright side; this is the perfect opportunity to update your wardrobe."

Eyeing the full English fry-up longingly Barry decided he daren't risk the grease triggering his travel sickness, instead breakfasting on muesli washed down with a glassful of vinegar and local honey. Marigold announced that from now on we would breakfast on village bread, olives and muesli as she didn't appreciate the smell of a fry-up lingering in the new kitchen. She didn't appear too amused by my quip that the invasive stench of Maria burning plastic would soon dispel the smell of fried bacon.

BUCKET TO GREECE

Clutching his flask full of the local travel sickness remedy Barry prepared for the off. Marigold, overcome with tears as we waved him goodbye, retired indoors to fix her mascara, thus failing to notice the removal van coming to a stop at the other end of the village street, inconveniently blocking the narrow road whilst Barry exchanged tender kisses of farewell with Cynthia. Only the persistent honk of Greek horns finally parted them. Reflecting that Marigold would be kicking herself if she knew she'd missed the chance to spy on her brother's budding romantic entanglement, I decided to keep quiet.

Unfortunately my good intentions to spare my wife's feelings were thwarted when Harold put in an unwanted appearance, barging uninvited into the house and immediately launching into a loud complaint about the Greek labourer who'd been working on our house publicly canoodling with that English man-eating hussy Cynthia from the olive grove.

"But Vangelis is a married man," Marigold proclaimed in shock, momentarily forgetting that Barry had passed himself off as a non-English speaking labourer to avoid conversing with

Harold and his ghastly wife.

I was appalled that Harold had the temerity to not only stride into our house uninvited, but to slanderously disparage the yet to be met Cynthia as a hussy: Spiros had spoken very highly of her and I trusted his judgement far more than that of the blithering idiot who'd barged into my home. My brief acquaintance with the dreadful overbearing boorish man assured me he was certainly no judge of character. Owing absolutely no explanation to Harold regarding my brother-in-law's recent connection with Cynthia, I sent Marigold a warning look not to engage with him.

Before I could stop him, Harold rudely pushed me out of the way, no easy feat since I towered above him, his obvious chunkiness lending strength to his diminutive stature. Striding from the entrance hallway into the newly renovated grand salon he gave the room a curt onceover, snidely commenting, "You've certainly got your work cut out for you here. I can see the old fellow who snuffed it had horrible taste."

Biting my tongue I watched in amazement as he marched into the kitchen, helping himself to a stray slice of bacon from Barry's neglected breakfast plate, saying, "Bacon, I don't mind if I do."

I gleefully waited for Harold to get his comeuppance; he would soon discover the neglected breakfast had been treated to a generous spray of pine scented air freshener, a cunning trick I had employed to not only appease Marigold by disguising the smell, but to deter Cynthia's vile mutant cat from licking the plate if it had the audacity to stage yet another break-in.

"Good God, this Greek bacon is foul," he spat. "You just can't get decent bacon in this country, there'll be hell to pay if you've gone and given me food poisoning."

"I'm afraid that's the risk you took when you engaged in the filthy habit of helping yourself to uncovered leftovers left out at room temperature, it's a repugnantly unhygienic practice," I ridiculed, barely able to contain my delight at his horror.

Harold appeared shocked by my reprimand. I presumed he didn't have many friends to stand up to him, and our earlier encounter had demonstrated he was used to talking down to his wife in his superior manner; quite ironic considering Joan stood a head taller than him. While the cat had his tongue I took the chance to belittle him further by launching into a long and tedious list of all the possible strains of food poisoning he had potentially exposed himself to with his greed, hoping to bore him into leaving. His face turned progressively redder as I recited the words 'campylobacter enteritis, Escherichia coli, salmonella and staphylococcus', even throwing in 'ciguatera' for good measure, knowing he'd be far too ignorant to realise it was impossible to contract fish poisoning from air freshened bacon. I ended my deliberately tedious lecture by suggesting he hot foot it to the pharmacy and invest in a good emetic, and just to be on the safe side, a fast acting laxative.

"Good God you doctors really like to paint a bleak picture," he finally snorted, having erroneously presumed I was a medical professional due my extensive knowledge of foodborne illnesses. Clutching his stomach he pushed past me, uttering the final words, "Don't bother trying to bill me, I know what rip-off merchants you doctors are."

Unable to resist tormenting him further I called out some last minute advice as he rushed down the stairs. "You might like to try the local remedy of a glassful of vinegar and honey."

"Oh Victor, you are awful," Marigold chuckled as we headed onto the balcony together to watch Harold make a desperate dash towards the pharmacy.

Chapter 21

**Your Prime Minister is
Very Handsome**

Vangelis put in a late appearance that morning, completely understandable when he explained, "I saw the Harold come visiting so to avoid the detestable man I go for the coffee. By the, how you say, the luck of the drawer, I find an old gate in the good condition. You will like, it is full of how you say, the character. It will be the excellent barrier to keeping the Harold out. You want I to fix it now Victor, before tiling?"

"It was certainly a stroke of luck to come across a suitable gate Vangeli," I said, delighted I wouldn't have to shell out for a brand new one, knowing I could sell Marigold on second-hand if it did indeed add character to the property.

"Unfortunately keeping Harold out will have to wait, we have a more pressing matter. Water was pouring into the hallway from the roof terrace last night in the rain, would you mind taking a look."

"That is not good. I will look now; I hope I can find the point of entry to make the house waterproof."

Whilst Vangelis investigated the terrace for possibly leaky entrance points I decided to dedicate a few hours to the Greek phrase book. If Guzim made another impromptu visit bearing free fruit I wanted to be ready with some pre-prepared memorised phrases. Although all of the phrases were definitely out-dated and appeared of no practical value in the course of normal conversation, I persevered, thinking if nothing else the exercise provided an opportunity to perfect my pronunciation. By morning's end I had committed to memory the Greek for 'your prime minister is very handsome', 'do you play the bagpipes?', 'my wife is a vegetarian but plays the piano very well', and 'a sheep has eaten our sandwiches'.

I considered the last phrase could potentially be useful if I perhaps substituted the word sheep for goat, since the borrowed creature was still chomping its way through our undergrowth. I decided it wouldn't do to spread blatant lies about Marigold since she was neither a vegetarian nor a proficient piano player, but considered the bagpipe phrase might come in handy if I happened across a Greek who had holidayed in Scotland. I thought it was a bit rich to go around proclaiming the prime minister of Albania was very handsome when I had no clue who held the position and wouldn't even be able to pick him out a line-up. Tossing the book aside in frustration I headed up to the roof terrace to pick Vangelis' brain. With no hesitation he immediately provided the name of the Albanian prime minister.

"Seriously, Fatos Nano?" I said.

BUCKET TO GREECE

"Is quite apt Victor," Vangelis laughed, indicating by sweeping his hands over his belly that Mr Nano was of generous girth.

"And do you consider him a handsome chap?" I asked.

"Really Victor, that kind of thing, the beauty of the man, is a matter of the personal taste. For me, I could never to find the socialist attractive, being a member of the New Democracy. But tell me Victor, do you consider the Konstantinos Simitis to be handsome?"

"I have no clue who that is," I admitted.

"He is the Prime Minister of Greece, and not, I think, attractive. Here in *Ellada* we take the pride in our politics. I believe it would be good for you to acquaint yourself with the important figures and the political parties, and worry the less about their good looks," Vangelis advised, his eyes twinkling with amusement despite the serious expression plastered on his face.

Hoping to convince Vangelis I was in fact a man of substance rather than someone only concerned with superficialities, I attempted to impress him with my practiced Greek, saying "*O prothypourgos sas einai omorfos.*"

"He really isn't Victor, the prime minister is bald and weedy," Vangelis retorted, adding, "But your Greek pronunciation is coming on the nicely, I understood you easily."

Later that day Marigold and I enjoyed a pleasant stroll through the village, venturing up roughly cobbled steep alleyways, pondering if shutters were closed for siesta time or if the properties were empty, and their owners perhaps toiling away in the cities. We marvelled at old wooden doors with paint peeling away, yet furnished with elegantly crafted door knobs fashioned in the style of hands or lions' mouths. We wondered what secrets were hidden behind arched entranceways and how the crumbling curved stones stayed so solidly in place.

Marigold coveted the exquisite lacework concealing alley facing windows and said we must look out for some on our shopping trip. We clambered up winding stone steps, worn with the tread of possible ancients, tripping over ubiquitous cats we disturbed from their mid-afternoon slumbers. We inhaled the rich aroma of oregano and garlic, the heady scent of Greek cooking. We derived pleasure from each simple thing, captivated by the charms of our newly adopted village, reaffirming we had made the right decision in moving to this wonderful land.

"No regrets?" I asked Marigold as we stopped in the shade of a fig tree to share a kiss.

"No regrets at all," she replied.

Chapter 22

Pilfering, Parking and Poodles

It seemed that the hours spent studying the practically obsolete Greek phrasebook had been to no avail since there was no sign of Guzim bearing free fruit the next morning. I took my wife coffee in bed, reminding her we needed an early start as were taking the two cats up to the vet in town to finally be spayed.

I was taken by surprise when Guzim eventually came knocking since it was already daylight and thus far all our encounters had occurred under the cover of darkness. After exchanging greetings we made the by now obligatory swap; a cap full of plump purple figs so perfectly ripe they were spilling their rich juices, in return for a chilled bottle of Amstel. As Guzim guzzled the beer I took the opportunity to tell him in my studied Greek, "Your Prime Minister, Fatos Nano, is very handsome."

His blank stare was a good indication that I had failed to impress him so I robotically repeated the memorised phrase, not once but twice, concentrating carefully on my pronunciation to ensure my Greek was comprehensible. This time Guzim responded by turning aside and spitting over the stair rail, a reaction I interpreted as spitting in the face of socialism. Refusing to see my hours of study go to waste I soldiered on, telling him 'a sheep has eaten our sandwiches' but cleverly substituting the word sheep for goat in deference to our borrowed weed eater. This time my words garnered a strong reaction, with Guzim repeating the word sandwich, flashing his toothless smile whilst nodding vigorously. Indicating he should wait one moment I dashed into the kitchen and speedily prepared a cheese and onion sandwich for him, careful to remove the crust in consideration of his lack of teeth. If truth be told he looked like he could do with a decent meal.

It proved difficult to continue our chat since Guzim's mouth was now stuffed full of sandwich, leaving me no choice other than to continue on in a one-sided conversation. In desperation I resorted to asking him if he played the bagpipes, thinking I really must invest in a more up-to-date phrase book. Guzim's response was to shake his head slowly from side to side before making a speedy exit down the stairs, not even bothering to exchange good-byes or thank me for the sandwich.

"I'm beginning to think our shed dweller lacks basic manners," I complained to Marigold as she sauntered into the kitchen, smartly dressed in tailored shorts for our trip to town. "He practically demanded a sandwich to go with his beer, and then legged it with not so much as a by-your-leave," I exaggerated.

"I'm afraid to say he's been playing you for a fool Victor," she said.

"How so?" I asked, confused by her words.

"I was in the spare bedroom looking for the cat basket when I happened to see a shabbily dressed man plucking the fruit from a fig tree in the garden. I was about to call out 'thief' when it occurred to me it must be your friendly shed dweller. He's been slyly gifting you with your very own figs every morning and you've been gullibly repaying his false kindness with free beer."

"I'd completely forgotten we even had a fig tree," I obfuscated to cover my embarrassment at being had. "We really do need to start work on the garden and take a full inventory of what is growing out there."

"And you seriously need to speak to Spiros about the Albanian in the shed, pilfering our produce is just not on," Marigold said.

"Well in fairness he did hand it over after picking it, so technically he didn't pilfer any-thing. Perchance I misinterpreted the situation; I did rather jump to the conclusion that he was making a gift of the figs. Perhaps he was angling for some work in the garden, communicating with him can be a bit of a minefield," I replied, explaining I remained totally flummoxed as to whether or not Guzim was working far away from home to support a multitude of children, chickens or wives.

"You're right about the garden, we really must think about making a start, but right now we have a more pressing problem. I can only find one cat basket; I can't think what has happened to the other one."

"Barry had it, he used it to return that vile mutant to Cynthia," I recalled. "I expect he forgot to bring it back."

"He probably had other things on his mind when he left her house the other evening," Marigold winked. "We can't possibly shove two drugged cats into one basket, you'll have to go round there now Victor and get the other one back."

"I hope she's at home," I said worriedly. I had already fed the cats their breakfast laced with crushed sedatives and needed to basket them up quickly before their tranquilised state wore off and they got their claws out.

Like Marigold, Cynthia appeared not to be a morning person, answering the door in her dressing gown and looking at me cautiously through bleary eyes. Her glossy brunette hair resembled a bird's nest, leading me to suppose I'd dragged her out of bed. Hoping she didn't

suspect I was the type of early morning gentle-
man caller bearing fruit in exchange for beer, I
hastily introduced myself, explaining the pre-
dicament of the missing cat basket.

"Of course, I'm so sorry, I did intend to return it yesterday; in fact I was on my way over
to yours with it when I saw that you had a visi-
tor and I didn't like to intrude," Cynthia said,
elaborating with the single word "Harold"
when I protested I couldn't recall receiving any
visitors.

"Phhh, that pushy oik has acquired the
habit of turning up uninvited," I said, thinking I
must remind Vangelis to fix the gate in place
now that he'd sorted the leak; and wondering if
it was too soon in my acquaintance with Cynthia to regale her with the account of how I'd got
shot of the dreadful man with dire predictions
of the gross foodborne illnesses he could expect
to be afflicted with after filching air-freshened
leftover bacon.

"Do come in, I'll get the basket," Cynthia invited, adding, "Would you like coffee?"

Recalling Harold's nasty words maligning
Cynthia as a man-eating hussy I politely declined, suddenly aware that curtains were

twitching in neighbouring houses and not wishing to risk besmirching her reputation further.

"I'm in a bit of a hurry I'm afraid, the cats are already drugged up and if it starts to wear off we'll have a dreadful time getting them into their baskets," I apologised.

"Oh I know, it's a terrible business getting them to the vet, they can sense these things," Cynthia said, passing me the basket. "Why don't you and your wife call round later for a drink, you'll certainly need one after a trip to the vet. It will give us a chance to get acquainted."

"Excellent," I agreed, thinking if Marigold and I arrived together it wouldn't feed the gossip.

This was our first trip up to town with me at the wheel of the Punto, rather than travelling as passengers in Spiros' hearse. I drove with great caution, wary of the erratic behaviour of other road users who appeared disinclined to show the same respect to the Punto as they would to the hearse. Other drivers discourteously tailgated the Punto, waiting for an opportune moment to overtake, a risky business considering the sheer number of hair-pin bends on the mountainous road. I was forced to slam the brakes on hard when a car approached in my lane, seemingly heading for a head-on collision but mercifully slipping in front of the coach it was overtaking with only inches to spare. I was able to recover my composure when a herd of sheep and goats crossing the road in a straggly and leisurely procession brought traffic to a grinding halt in both directions.

"You don't get that on the A6," Marigold commented, waving cheerily to the shepherd as I restarted the engine following the ten minute hold-up.

Spiros had always eschewed the central car park on our trips to town, scoffing that no one in their right mind paid for parking when there were perfectly good streets available for free. Spiros firmly believed the advent of pay and display car parks in Greece was yet another sign of the slippery start of some European Union calculated conspiracy to encroach on centuries of Greek tradition. He liked to press the point by saying, "Before you know it they'll be trying to ban smoking and open bottles of olive oil on restaurant tables." Spiros was a sucker for any half-baked and far-fetched conspiracy theory.

Being of obviously unsound mind I headed straight to the car park, having no intention of polluting the atmosphere with unnecessary fumes that could pose a health and safety menace by driving round and round in endless circles, navigating side streets clogged with double-parked cars. Some of the drivers even had the audacity to actually park on the pavements, disregarding the obstructive hazard this lazy habit presented to pedestrians.

It appeared Spiros' attitude to paying for parking was shared by many other Greeks since the car park proved to be near empty. Spotting a couple of cars sporting GB number plates I surmised the car park was mainly the preserve of foreigners; presumably they shared my sensible opinion that forking out a couple of euros on parking fees represented a saving on the petrol expended on driving aimlessly around for hours, searching for a space.

"I don't know why you couldn't have just found a convenient parking space nearby," Marigold complained when we finally reached our destination, hot and sweaty from lugging two cats in their heavy baskets, for twenty minutes on foot.

"Look, there's a space almost right outside the door."

"Let me just find a hanky to wipe the sweat from my brow before we go in," I pleaded, hoping no one would notice if I discreetly swiped said hanky over my now damp armpits.

"I told you that you'd get overheated in that outfit Victor, you should have worn shorts and a short sleeved shirt."

"I didn't want to stand out as a tourist," I reminded her. Failing to find a convenient hanky I resorted to wiping the sweat from my brow with the end of my tie, before adjusting said tie beneath my sleeveless pullover to conceal the now evident damp patch. I reflected that Marigold was right and my attire of a long sleeved shirt and long trousers wasn't really suitable for traipsing round town in the heat. Marigold had her own qualms about venturing out in public in shorts since her legs were still white and they didn't appear to stock fake tan in the village shop. Her qualms were dispelled when she realised that white legs must be all the fashion as the most elegant Greek women took great pains to keep out of the sun. Still, apart from the odd tourist in town, Marigold was the only woman wearing shorts, the Greeks already moving onto their winter wardrobes as the first signs of autumn appeared.

"We have to acclimatise Victor; you can't expect to just turn Greek overnight."

The veterinarian's office didn't appear to work on either an appointment or ticket system. We hesitantly entered a waiting room full of people and a motley assortment of animals: I use that description deliberately since most of them could hardly be considered cute pets. A couple of ferocious looking guard dogs snarled threateningly at our arrival, straining at their leashes to snap their dribbling jaws in the face of our cats. A piglet snorted in one corner, objecting to the too-small cat basket it had been caged in. A muscly young man with long wavy black hair and heavy metal tattoos, kitted out in black motor cycle leathers, was bizarrely accompanied by a pampered pet poodle, ridiculously coiffed with shiny pink bows. A middle-aged woman with a bored expression clutched a cardboard box on her lap, piquing my curiosity as to what type of creature was concealed inside.

With no receptionist to guide us we took our cue to sit down when the other patrons shuffled up to make room for us. Apart from the animal noises, the room was silent; everyone pretending not to stare following the obligatory exchange of greeting.

"We could be in for a long wait," Marigold hissed.

"Ah, you are English," the tattooed motor-cyclist piped up. "This must confuse you; your country is famous for the orderly queue. It is something to emulate indeed, but I fear us Greeks would not be receptive to it. No doubt the European Union will try to foist the queuing system upon us by law, but Greeks will resist."

"Yes, it is a tad confusing without an appointment system," I concurred, surmising the poodle owner was another sucker for a good conspiracy theory; he would no doubt get on like a house on fire with Spiros.

"Let me advise you how you must handle this," he said, leaning in close to whisper, "As soon as the vet opens the door to the treatment room you must rush forward and thrust your cat in his face. That way he knows which turn to give you."

"Have you been waiting long?" Marigold asked him.

"Too long for Fufu, she is getting restless," he sighed. At the mention of its name the pampered pouch started yapping relentlessly, attracting if looks-could-kill glares from everyone in the packed waiting room. "I'm in next after the cardboard box and one turn before the pig."

Following his advice I kept a beady eye on the surgery door, ready to pounce and stake my claim to an allotted spot as soon as it opened. The door was finally opened by a white-coated jovial man in his thirties and I leapt forward to show him the basketed Clawsome. Acknowledging with a nod that he had noted my presence, he indicated I should return to my seat. Stepping to one side he held the door wide to make room for the patient he had been attending to make its exit. No one apart from Marigold and I blinked an eye at the surreal sight of a donkey being led out of the inner sanctum. The veterinarian then perused the people waiting their turn with a calculating eye. Blithely ignoring the bored woman with the cardboard box who was supposedly next up, he pointed to the young man in leathers and waved him inside.

Catching my eye the middle-aged woman with the cardboard box shrugged her shoulders

in resignation, saying "*O skulos*," which I understood meant dog. She stopped short, presuming
as foreigners we couldn't understand, instead
using her hands to mimic the motion of yapping
to finish her point. We nodded in agreement, as-
suming the poodle had been allowed to jump
the queue to put an end to its ear-splitting yapping.

Finally entering the treatment room I consulted
the piece of paper retrieved from my pocket on
which I'd scrawled the necessary vocabulary to
communicate the purpose of our visit, telling
the vet in faltering Greek what turned out to be,
"spayed the cats need I."

"Tell me in English," he encouraged, to my
great relief. I explained that we needed both cats
sterilising as there was a predatory Tom on the
loose with designs on their virtue.

After examining the still docile cats the vet
announced, "I think you are too late to save the
virtue of this one, she is already pregnant."

"How on earth could that have happened?"
Marigold asked rhetorically, since she was well
acquainted with the facts of life.

"It's obvious, that mutant of Cynthia's has

managed to have its way with Clawsome," I stated.

"Oh Clawsome," Marigold sighed, her face plastered in disappointment as though our pet was a recalcitrant teenage girl who'd disobeyed her, sneaking off behind the bike shed to get up to unspeakable things with an unsuitable boy despite all her best warnings.

"I can spay the other one, but if we do the pregnant one it will kill the unborn kittens," the vet advised.

"We can't allow that," Marigold cried. "Just do Catastrophe for now; we'll have Clawsome seen to once she's delivered."

"Are you prepared to welcome a houseful of kittens?" I asked. "Surely two cats are enough trouble as it is."

"How can you be so heartless Victor, of course she must be allowed to birth her kittens. If she has quite a brood I'm sure we can find some of them good homes in the village."

"If there are so many good homes with open doors then why are the streets of Meli knee-deep in strays?" I asked.

"But Clawsome's offspring will be of good pedigree," Marigold protested as though this social cachet would give them an automatic entry into village homes.

"Dubious pedigree at best," I scoffed, presuming if Cynthia's cat was indeed the culprit behind Clawsome's situation any resultant kittens would undoubtedly be monstrous looking mutants.

"Don't worry, first time mothers usually have no more than two or three," the vet said. "Try not to give her any more sedatives in her condition; you don't want to risk having drugged-up kittens."

Chapter 23

Something Fishy

I suspected Marigold was secretly delighted by the news our current menagerie of pets would soon be doubled and that she had absolutely no intention of parting with any of the litter. After leaving the veterinarian she worried about abandoning the pregnant cat in the car whilst we went off on a shopping spree, so we decided to delay our jaunt around the shops until we could return to town cat free. Knowing how much I'd been looking forward to our first trip to the market she suggested we could run round the stalls quickly, a token gesture to appease me for not opposing her decision to spare the kittens from the scalpel.

"We'll have to get a move on," I said. "Vangelis told me they start packing up the *agora* around noon."

Marigold soon forgot all about the cats slumbering in their baskets in the car with the windows left ajar, enthralled by the sights, sounds and heady smells of the open market. Even though it was close to noon the place was still packed with crowds milling round the heaped stalls, sited below colourful sun canopies. There was so much fresh produce on sale, stalls spilling over with plump peppers in every hue of green, red, orange and yellow. We were tempted by fat purple aubergines, onions with translucent red skins, and odd shaped carrots still sprouting green tops that Tesco quality control would surely reject out of hand as aberrations despite their obvious freshness. Stalls were piled high with courgettes, tomatoes and cucumbers, all at ridiculously low prices. There were green and red apples, succulent bunches of red and green grapes, luscious green and purple figs, and watermelons too big to carry.

"There's so much choice," Marigold exclaimed, examining the coins she needed in order to hand over the correct change for two kilos of aubergines.

"It's amazing," I agreed, restraining Marigold from snapping up a bag of fresh figs with the reminder that we had a tree full of the things at home.

I was surprised that I couldn't find a fresh basil plant anywhere but fortunately the phrase book provided me with the necessary word, allowing me to enquire where I could get my hands on some *vasilikos*. My enquiry was met with numerous shrugs until one stall holder took pity me on me, telling me in broken English, "No eat, it flower, buy in flower shop."

"How completely bizarre," I commented to Marigold.

"You've probably mixed up the word Victor, whoever heard of flower shops selling kitchen herbs," Marigold said, rolling her eyes. She changed her tune when she spotted an area off to one side of the market filled with pots of flowering plants. Knowing Marigold could never resist a flowering pot plant I spotted her ulterior motive in suggesting we go for a closer look on the off-chance they sold basil. Not sharing her interest in flowering plants I wandered off, intrigued by the sight of a push-cart laden with nothing but garlic bulbs. It was manned by a thin boy in his early teens, his eyes constantly darting in all directions as though in fear of something. I wondered if his garlic was on wheels to perhaps facilitate a speedy departure if the market inspector turned up to examine his presumably non-existent permit.

Returning to my wife I had to physically restrain her from shelling out the best part of fifty euros on unnecessary flowering plants. "There'll be plenty of time to buy this kind of thing once the garden is in order," I reasoned.

"But I have chosen these to add a splash of colour to the roof terrace," she argued.

I knew that if I sanctioned her frivolous purchase it would only be the start of her flower related expenditure, correctly guessing she would soon demand every plant currently housed in plastic tubs be transplanted into expensive ceramic ones. She finally settled on just four of the plants, but only because she was worried about fitting them all into the car with the cats. Needless to say the flower sellers didn't have a single pot of basil between them, confirming I would need to look in a flower shop rather than the market.

Weighed down with fruit and vegetables, we hauled our purchases to the car before setting off for round two, an exploration of the indoor food market, forced to walk single file in the crowded space between heaped stalls lining each side of the walkway. Here large plastic jars full of home prepared olives and plastic bottles of olive oil were on sale beside freshly grown produce and fragrant bunches of dried herbs and tea. It was interesting to note the difference in prices between the same types of produce. I made a mental note that next time we should make a full tour of the market before buying anything, to ensure we took advantage of the best prices for the most appealing produce.

The walkway split off to one side, leading into the meat market. Huge sides of pig hung from metal hooks and burly looking chaps in blood stained aprons hacked at vast slabs of meat with cleavers, the smoke spiralling from the cigarettes clamped between their lips no distraction from their concentration. I nudged Marigold to draw her attention to a fat cockerel suspended upside down, feet still intact and tied together; "You don't get many of those in Tesco."

"If it's all the same I'll give it a miss, I prefer my fowl feetless," she quipped.

The path we were following meandered past quaint little market shops stocked with a rich variety of cheese, ouzo, dried beans and any other number of things from roughhewn chunks of olive oil soap to jars of thyme scented honey and salt packed pieces of dried bakaliaros. We watched in amusement as fresh eggs were slipped into paper bags, not a traditional egg box in sight, confident they would be carried home with their delicate shells intact.

The strong smell of fish alerted me to our proximity to the fish market, an area I couldn't wait to explore. Large open crates of every conceivable type of fish sat on ice, ranging in size from the smallest gavros to veritable monster sized swordfish, all staring at us with cold dead eyes. Since we'd had no kitchen until now we had been dining on things easy to prepare, mainly bread, olives, tomatoes, cheese and tzatziki purchased from the village store. By now I was all tzatzikied out on the rich garlic and cu-

cumber yoghurt dip and was most definitely in the mood for some fresh fish. Even the cats were tzatzikied out, Clawsome regarding me with as much disdain as though I had just devoured her first new-born when I piled the dip into her feeding bowl, unaware she was repulsed by the smell of garlic.

Although each type of fish was labelled I was unable to understand any of the lettering of the Greek script beyond the price. Naturally I could recognise basics such as octopus, squid, prawns and crayfish, but the whole fish that interested me mostly remained a mystery; and the fishmonger whose produce I decided to make my selection from couldn't help me out with any English. Nevertheless the transaction was conducted successfully through sign language and I walked away the proud owner of two large whole fish which the fish monger patiently sounded out as *lavraki*.

"Don't expect me to have anything to do with them," Marigold said in a steely tone. "I'm used to buying my fish already filleted from Tesco. I'd have no clue where to start decapitating and gutting those slimy things."

"Leave it to me Marigold; I intend to cook

you a wonderful fish dinner this evening. You don't spend as much time as I have in restaurant kitchens without picking up a thing or two about scaling and preparing whole fish."

Strolling back to the car with our purchases we were delighted to run into Spiros. As we gushed about how wonderful the market was he asked if there was something fishy in my bags. Despite my bluster about having no problem with tackling fully intact fish I felt rather stupid when Spiros pointed out that the fishmonger would have happily gutted the *lavraki* for me if only I'd gestured a signal.

Chapter 24

A Pregnant and Gay Misunderstanding

Spiros of course insisted we join him for coffee when we bumped him into him at the market. Marigold for once prevaricated about accepting the invitation, worried about leaving the cats cooped up alone for any longer.

"I really think we ought to be heading back to the village. Don't think of me as a worrywart Spiro, but the heat is getting to us and we have just found out we are about to become new parents," she proudly announced, thoughtlessly omitting any reference to the cat.

"Ah, the wonders of the modern science," Spiros exclaimed, politely attempting to hide his shocked incredulity that Marigold could possibly still be fertile. Admittedly my wife looks remarkably good for her age, but it would be stretching the laws of nature if she managed to get pregnant. Spiros belatedly feigned congratulations, his sceptical eyes fixated on Marigold's stomach in stunned disbelief.

"What Marigold meant to say is that we have just found out one of the cats is pregnant," I explained. "We have them cooped up in the car."

"They'll be fine, we take them with us," Spiros boomed, obviously greatly relieved that nature and science had not after all been in cahoots to trick him. "Victor, you follow me in the Punto, I not want the cat hairs in the hearse."

I hadn't realised the invitation to coffee would involve driving somewhere else, having presumed we'd pop into the perfectly adequate looking cafe adjacent to the market. My suggestion that we take coffee in the more conveniently placed establishment was met with derision by

Spiros proclaiming, "Victor what are you to thinking? What if Marigold need the toilet, an elegant woman such as she will not appreciate the Turkish hole in the floor in that place. No, we go to the marina, it have the modern toilet and the fresh sea air for the cats."

The fresh sea air wafted in through the open windows of the plush coffee bar overlooking the marina. Spiros and I sipped iced coffees, whilst Marigold got slowly squiffy on the fancy cocktail Spiros treated her to, saying she deserved an alcoholic treat to toast becoming a new parent, even if it was a surrogate one to the cat.

The up-market surroundings made me glad I had turned out in a tie, even if it had proved a sweaty encumbrance earlier. The opulent splendour of the luxury yachts moored at the marina attracted both our admiration and envy.

"My uncle he always dream he be the next Onassis with the fine yacht," Spiros shared, "but sadly the nearest he got was swabbing out the deck of the fish trawler."

"What brought you up to town this morning Spiro?" I asked.

"The haircut. I not trust the village barber,

he give everyone the same short back and sides, but never to finish properly the back. You look closely; you will see every man in the village has the lopsided neckline."

"Well your haircut is lovely Spiro, not a trace of an uneven neckline," Marigold gushed, obviously beginning to feel the effects of the cocktail.

"It's a long way to come for a haircut," I pointed out.

"Well I have the date tonight and wish to make, how you say, the good first impression."

"A date, how exciting," Marigold trilled, blatantly fishing for more information.

"It is with a tourist woman I met on the beach, I think my magnificent physique attracted her. She is from the England," he confided.

"Oh, not with Cynthia then?" I asked, hoping to ascertain Spiros' interest had moved on, thus leaving the field free for Barry without any awkwardness ensuing between the two men. Recalling the rich and bloody history of protracted feuds in the Mani, the last thing I wanted was to be called as a second if Spiros challenged Barry to a duel between rival lovers at dawn.

"The Cynthia tell me straight, Spiro she say 'I cannot to love the undertaker.' I understand, many many the woman have the same reaction, they cannot separate the repulsion they feel for my business with the dead bodies, from me, Spiros, the man. My wife say the reason she divorce me is I always bring the smell of the embalming fluid to the bed. The English tourist not care how I make the living, she just want some fun with the handsome Greek. Many of your countrymen take the holiday to flirt with the men; we have the reputation for the best lovers in the world," Spiros boasted.

"There's nothing like false modesty," I laughed, surprised to learn Spiros had been married.

Marigold excused herself to use the Spiros approved toilet and I broached the subject of basil, curious if my faltering Greek had led me to misunderstand the absurdity of basil plants only being available for sale in flower shops.

"You want the *vasilikos* plant Victor, why you not to tell me? I give to you; I have the many; do not to pay the rip-off price in the flower shop. Soon you will to grow your own."

"That's most generous of you Spiro, but I'm

still curious why such a popular cooking herb isn't for sale at the market alongside other herbs," I pressed.

"The Greek not like to eat the sacred *vasilikos*, it have the orthodox association with the, how to say in translate, the rising of the holy cross the Jesus was crucified on," Spiros explained. "I do not share this superstitious belief and freely eat the *vasilikos* with the feta; the sweetness compliments the saltiness to perfection."

Agreeing that the flavours of feta and basil married well together I persisted: "But why does every house in Meli have a pot of the stuff on the doorstep if Greeks don't eat it?"

"They have for the ornament, and the good luck," Spiros said. Looking around to confirm Marigold was still in the toilet and not within earshot he added, "I would not like to embarrass the Marigold after my earlier misunderstanding about her implausible fecundity, but the *vasilikos* is lucky for the fertility. When Vangelis has made all the finish on your house we must to get the Papas in to give the blessing, he uses the *vasilikos* to sprinkle the holy water."

On her return Marigold reminded me that I

must grill Spiros about the Albanian living in the stone shed in our garden. In truth I was a tad wary about bringing up this potentially thorny matter. My confusion remained after speaking to Vangelis as to whether he'd meant Guzim was in Greece illegally, or if the sale of the stone shed to Guzim had been conducted under the table with illegal undertones. I would hate for Spiros to imagine I thought he had been involved in anything underhand, but perturbed that no mention of the strange shed set-up had been alluded to in the legal papers signed when we exchanged contracts.

"My uncle sell the stone shed to the Guzim and the land it sit on, and I think, another the fifty centimetres around it so he have the space to the put chair in the sunshine," Spiros said. "I tell my uncle this is the awkward arrangement to sell, how you say, just a piece of the garden, but he find the lawyer to make it all legal."

"So not the entirety of the garden at the back of our house actually belongs to us?" I clarified.

"That is so. You did not buy nor own the piece of garden with the shed. I tell to the uncle that selling the piece of garden to the Guzim would complicate matters if he ever wanted to sell the house, but he insist he will live there till he die. I think he not anticipate he will die so soon, but still the garden division and the sale of the shed was all legal," Spiros said.

I was relieved that Guzim's shed was technically nothing to do with me. He'd bought it fair and square, and wasn't squatting in my garden. It all sounded complicated but legit, until Spiros added; "All is legal except for the Guzim, who is the illegal in Greece."

I mulled Spiros' words over; astonished by the artful tactics a devious lawyer had seemingly employed in order to facilitate the legal sale of a plot of land complete with stone shed, to an illegal alien. I recalled spotting the stone shed from the roof terrace on our first viewing of the house. When I had asked Spiros about it he had replied: "No, that is not part of the property, unless you can persuade the Guzim to sell it." I had thought no more of it at the time.

I had no wish to be perceived as an arrogant foreigner, moving to Greece only to turf an Albanian who had been settled here much longer than me, out of his rightful home. I had no intention of using Guzim's illegal status to bring any trouble to his doorstep; the inconvenience of him living at the bottom of my garden did not justify his deportation. Guzim had every legal right to live in the shed if the authorities didn't cotton on to the fact that he was actually living in Greece illegally, and we would hardly miss the tiny square of land it stood on since the garden was huge. The only problem was the clear lack of access from the shed, and Marigold's objection to being exposed to Guzim conducting his ablutions under the hosepipe. As I voiced these thoughts to Spiros an idea occurred to me.

"If we erect a high wooden fence around the stone shed it will serve as a clear demarcation between the land he purchased and ours, at the same time affording Guzim privacy should he choose to get naked under the hosepipe," I suggested.

"This is the excellent idea Victor, *bravo*," Spiros agreed.

"And if we make an opening in the wall next to the shed Guzim will have his very own access," I continued, delighted to have come up with a solution that would put an end to Guzim trooping through our garden or requiring a key for our new entry gate. I was happy to foot the cost of the fence and a hole in the wall new entrance as a viable solution that would not cause offence to Guzim.

"You are the good man Victor to think of this, not all the foreigns would give the consideration to the Guzim. I not like to talk badly about your countrymen but there is the disagreeable English man in Meli. In the same situation he would take the delight to exploit the problem and send the Guzim to deportation."

"You wouldn't be referring to Harold by any chance?" I asked.

"Yes, the Harold," Spiros confirmed. "A very difficult man, he have none of the refinement."

"I can assure you not all English people are like Harold, unfortunately his sort gives the rest of us a bad name."

"Yes, I know that well. The first time we meet Victor I know that you are the good man; that is why we are such the firm friends. It is kind of you to consider the Guzim when he tell to me that you are the mentally defective."

"Mentally defective?" I spluttered, outraged by the insult.

"Yes, either that or the gay, Guzim was not sure, he couldn't to make his mind up," Spiros said.

"How on earth did Guzim get the preposterous idea that Victor is gay, surely he realises he is a married man?" Marigold asked, choking back her laughter.

"Not that there's anything wrong with being gay, our son Benjamin is out and proud," I interjected.

"The Guzim thinks it is unnatural how attractive you find the Albanian Prime Minister, Fatos Nano. He say you obsess about how handsome he is. The Guzim thinks it is not natural to find the Fatos so beautiful."

"You find the Albanian prime minister attractive?" Marigold chortled, rolling her eyes in mirth.

"For goodness sake, I was practising my phrase book Greek on Guzim, how was I to know he'd get the wrong end of the stick," I said, wondering if perhaps my question about bagpipes had led him to believe I wasn't quite the full shilling. I supposed if someone had started rattling on to me about bagpipes and handsome prime ministers for no good reason I may have presumed they had a few loose marbles.

"It's a bit rich really for a blatant fig thief, who has the cheek to pass our own fruit off as a gift, to hurl insults around about Victor," Marigold said, suddenly worried word might spread that she was married to the village idiot who may start approaching the village men with unwanted advances.

"What is this about the figs?" Spiros asked.

"He's been giving me figs every morning and in return I give him a bottle of Amstel. I didn't realise he was giving me the figs from my own tree," I explained.

"I will speak to the Guzim about not helping himself to the fruit in your garden," Spiros promised. "Really, I am surprised he can spare any of the fruit he gives you since he sends all the money to the wife in Albania. He comes from the very poor country. It is very generous really of him to share your fruit with you, when he could simply have eaten it."

"We'd certainly have been none the wiser if he taken the fruit for himself. We certainly don't begrudge him a few figs, tell him to help himself if he's a bit hard up," I said.

"The Guzim could help you in the garden with the casual labour," Spiros suggested. "It will take many weeks for the goat you have borrowed to eat so many the weeds."

"Yes, I suppose we could come to some arrangement to give him a bit of work, though I'd appreciate you being there to translate when I suggest it," I agreed. "Perhaps you could also clear up the misunderstanding about my being infatuated with Fatos Nano. Did he happen to say anything else that was detrimental?"

"Oh no, he say you to make the most excellent sandwich, but please next time to leave the crusts on and not to scrimp so much on the onion," Spiros laughed.

Chapter 25

Cynthia's Rabbit Cat

We arrived back at the house in Meli to be greeted by Vangelis waving a paint brush at us from the roof terrace. We had decided to have the railings painted the same distinctly Greek blue as the balcony doors and window shutters; the fresh coat of paint Vangelis was applying really leant the place a distinguished air. I was delighted to see the old arched gate that Vangelis had found was now fixed securely in place. It was a definite find, the intricately scrolled bars adding imme-diate character and charm to the entrance.

"I think you should take Clawsome out of her basket, she needs the reassurance of human contact," Marigold said. The sedative had worn off and Clawsome had become agitated during the final approach to Meli. Holding the preg-nant cat close for comfort I rattled the gate, sur-prised to find Vangelis had locked us out. Un-fortunately because he'd also neglected to call down and warn me the paint was still wet, Clawsome's cream coat ended up decorated with a blue hand print.

"Sorry about that," Vangelis apologised, having rushed down from the roof terrace. Waving the new key to the gate in my face he said, "The Harold was on the prowl so I locked him out."

"Excellent thinking," I praised, before it dawned on me that if we hid from Harold be-hind the locked gate we'd be obliged to come outside and down the stairs to unlock the gate to admit any callers we didn't actually intend to deter.

"Perhaps Eduardo the electrician has the skills to hook the gate up as an electronic entrance," I suggested.

"You're working us," Vangelis retorted.

His odd choice of words led Marigold and I to exchange confused looks. Spotting our bewilderment Vangelis embellished his words by saying, "'You're working us' is the Greek idiom, like how you say in the English, 'you are taking the piss'."

"So in other words Eduardo isn't up to the job. Your idiom is far less crude. How do I say it in Greek, Vangeli?" I asked.

"*Eseis ergazeste emas.*"

"That's a bit of an alliterative tongue twister," I said, repeating the words in an effort to replicate Vangelis' pronunciation, and failing miserably.

"Was it not in your phrase book, Victor?" Vangelis enquired.

"No, the antiquated phrases in my book serve no useful purpose at all. My efforts to try them out on Guzim have only resulted in him spreading the word that I am both mentally defective and a homosexual."

"Not that there's anything wrong with being gay," Marigold hastened to add, "Our son Benjamin is proud and out."

"You will need to get spare keys to the gate cut in town Victor, the key is an old fashioned style," Vangelis said, speedily changing the subject, perhaps on the off chance I might ask for his reassurance that he thought I was normal.

"But we've only just driven all the way back from town," I pointed out, not eager to repeat the three-hour return journey, but aware that until we could sort Guzim out with a hole in the garden wall he would require a key. Without a key in the hands of the shed dweller we would be forced to either leave the gate unlocked or be on hand to cater to his every coming and going, and I knew from experience he kept very odd hours.

"We're not going back to town tomorrow, it's too much Victor. I need a rest after all that trailing around in the heat. We must simply leave the gate unlocked for the moment, after all you have come up with your own special way of dealing with Harold," Marigold said decisively. "Now we must hurry and get the shopping inside, Cynthia is expecting us for drinks and I can't wait to meet her and see for myself if she's Barry's perfect match. I've got the fish and fruit; you grab the bags of veggies Victor."

BUCKET TO GREECE

Cynthia greeted us warmly, leading us through to a tiny shaded patio area filled with flowering plants and furnished with a small table and chairs, unaware she was about to be subjected to an inquisitive grilling from Marigold. During the next thirty minutes my wife managed to prise out of Cynthia that she was a keen grecophile, having worked in the Greek tourist industry for several years in various regions of Greece. She had moved to the Mani just over two years ago, renting the small house in Meli. She utilised her growing language skills to secure steady employment as a tourist guide with a local travel agency in town that conducted coach trips to places of interest such as Athens, ancient Messene and Mystras. In the height of the tourist season she supplemented her income with a regular position greeting holidaymakers at the airport, dropping them off at their accommodation on the coast. She explained that because it was often more convenient to stay in town overnight between guided trips, her cats sometimes got out and went on the missing list.

I was under explicit instructions from my wife to absolutely not fire off any accusations that Cynthia's mutant grey Tom had ravished

Clawsome, leaving her pregnant, at least until the physical evidence clearly pointed in that direction. All bets were off though if Clawsome spawned some mini-replicas of the repugnant looking creature with the distinctive stripe. In spite of my promise to Marigold that I would hold my tongue, I could hardly contain myself when the ugly thing strutted onto the patio with all the flippant arrogance of a satisfied predator.

"Come to Mama, *Kouneli*," Cynthia pointlessly purred. It was patently obvious that the cat had no intention of responding, aloofly demonstrating absolutely no sign of attachment to her by turning its back in disdain.

"I thought *kouneli* was the Greek word for rabbit," I said, having spotted a totally useless rabbit related phrase in my archaic book. I tried to recall what it was, something along the line of 'are your rabbits breeding well for the season?' I wondered what had possessed Cynthia to name the Tom after a different type of mammal or if she had actually confused her mutant cat with a bunny.

"*Kouneli* is Greek for rabbit, it's the funniest thing; he had such a strange look about him when I discovered him abandoned under an olive tree that I actually mistook him for a rabbit. He was such a tiny mite, how anyone could abandon him I'll never know," Cynthia explained.

"Well he's been prowling round our female, sneaking into our house with the daring cunning of a practiced cat-burglar to sniff around her," I blurted out before Marigold could silence me with a withering look.

"Oh surely not, Kouneli already has a female companion, Buttercup. She's my other cat, Kouneli recently fathered her kittens, and they are just the cutest things, they popped out looking the spit of baby rabbits," Cynthia said. Her words made me wonder if Barry was aware she had the makings of a crazy cat lady.

"Barry's a great cat lover, isn't he Victor?" Marigold said, deftly attempting to steer the conversation onto her brother. "Of course our cats are recent additions to the family; it just wasn't practical keeping pets when we were both out at work all day. We only bought them before moving out here and Barry was really good about driving them over, wasn't he Victor?"

"I think Barry was a bit too nauseated to notice the cats," I pointed out.

"Oh, I heard all about the terrible problems he was having with travel sickness from all the old dears in the village, even before I met him. It's all they could talk about. They really took a shine to Barry, how they do love to make a fuss of him," Cynthia enthused; seemingly unaware she was in for a lot of competition if any of the village widows decided to catch themselves a new husband. "I do hope he doesn't suffer much on the drive back to England."

"Well I sent him off with a flask of vinegar and honey, apparently the local Greek remedy is very effective," I said.

"There's actually no such thing as a local Greek remedy for travel sickness," Cynthia laughed. "The old ladies made it up as an excuse to get chatting to him. I did give him some highly recommended travel sickness pills from the pharmacy though on the morning he left."

"You mean to say poor Barry has been ex-posing his insides to vinegar rot for no good purpose," I said in horror.

"Oh, it wouldn't make his insides rot," Cyn-thia contradicted. "Even if it was pointless drinking it as a cure for travel sickness Barry will have benefited from the placebo effect, not to mention vinegar is well renowned for lowering cholesterol, reducing belly fat and killing off all manner of nasty bacteria."

Cynthia's knowledge of nasty bacteria impressed me, convincing me she was a sensible woman who wouldn't take matters of food hygiene lightly. Marigold seemed equally impressed, having been won over by the fondness with which Cynthia spoke Barry's name. Out of the blue she suddenly invited Cynthia to join us for dinner that evening, telling her I could do wonderful things with the fresh *lavraki* we had bought at the market. Marigold's proposal that I pop back home and make a start on the cooking while they enjoyed a bit of a girly chat before joining me in an hour, was more of an order than a suggestion. I surmised Marigold had decided my presence could be dispensed with; she obviously intended to talk Barry up and didn't want me around to put my foot in it. Fortunately I was happy to comply, looking forward to cooking up a culinary masterpiece in the new kitchen.

Chapter 26

Guzim is Overcome

I decided I would prepare a traditional Greek appetiser of *melitzanosalata*, an aubergine salad, followed by pan seared *lavraki* with lemons served with a medley of Mediterranean vegetables: diced potatoes and peppers, shallots, olives and garlic, with fresh basil leaves adding the finishing touch. Visualising the dishes, I recalled with annoyance that I didn't have any basil. The realisation was immensely frustrating when I considered every doorstep in the village other than ours had a pot of the stuff standing sentinel outside. For just one moment I contemplated slyly raiding my neighbours' plants but I didn't want to get a reputation as the local basil thief. Instead I simply telephoned Spiros and reminded him he'd promised to give me a pot of the missing herb.

"I don't have much the time, I need to boot polish the hair before my date with the English tourist woman," Spiros said, handing over the basil plant five minutes later. Touched that he'd transplanted it into a handsome ceramic pot I persuaded him to come in for an ouzo whilst I prepared the salad, mindful it may be prudent to get rid of him before Cynthia turned up.

"Are you wining and dining your date at the local taverna?" I asked Spiros.

"Of course not, she would get the wrong idea and think I am the cheapskate," Spiros laughed. "I drive down to the coast to meet her and take her to the nice restaurant before I reel her in. Look, there is the Guzim coming home to his shed from the hard day's labour, we will speak to him Victor and tell him about your plans for the fence. No worry, I have the time, my hair not need the boot polish, I leave it natural."

"Don't forget to clear up that other matter of my being mentally defective," I reminded him

"And a homosexual," Spiros added with a wink.

Spiros and I joined Guzim at the bottom of the garden by the stone shed. Spiros immediately cleared up the misguided impression Guzim had formed of me by explaining it was all down to an unfortunate language mix up. Guzim rattled off a sentence that Spiros translated as the Albanian saying I must learn Greek; he had picked it up quickly through labouring and if he, an impoverished Albanian with no resources could manage it, then it should be a piece of cake for the rich foreigner. Guzim appeared hugely relived that Marigold was not after all a shield for my gayness, and that far from thinking Fatos Nano was a beautiful man I had never so much as clapped eyes on a picture of the esteemed fellow.

In turn Spiros was able to clarify that Guzim had just the one wife and three children, not thirteen. He didn't in fact keep any chickens in

Albania, preferring to breed rabbits. Spiros explained Guzim thought this the more sensible
option since chicken feathers didn't offer much
practical use, but once a rabbit was eaten its skin
was very useful for lining hole-ridden shoes.
Guzim's wife was apparently adept at weaving
loose rabbit fur into mittens and sweaters for the
children.

Guzim listened in awe as Spiros told him
about my plans to erect a tall fence around the
shed and to knock an entrance hole in the garden wall. He was overcome with emotion when
Spiros explained that I would be footing the bill
for these home improvements. Sinking to his
knees in gratitude, Guzim grasped my knees,
offering extravagant thanks in indecipherable
guttural Albanian. Tears of joy dripped down
Guzim's face as Spiros translated that the Albanian had always hoped to have his very own
fence one day, but had dismissed it as an impossible dream. A fence would allow him to wash
under the hosepipe in privacy, protected from
prying eyes.

"He is the modest man and not want the
Marigold gawping at his bits," Spiros said,
choking back laughter at very thought. "He is

happy a hole in the wall will not oblige him to trespass your garden."

Spiros went on to tell Guzim I was happy to have him help himself to any fruit and from now on he need not trouble to pick it for me. Guzim's face fell momentarily when he realised this new arrangement would put an end to the free bottle of Amstel, but perked up again when Spiros raised the subject of him doing some casual labouring in the garden to help me tame the wilderness into some sort of order. An arrangement was reached whereby Guzim would toil in the garden for three hours each evening at the end of his hard day's labouring; we shook on the princely sum of ten euros a day in wages.

Guzim's only request was that I pay him in cash on a daily basis. Apparently he'd done some work for Harold who had stitched him up over his wages, telling him he would be paid a lump sum at the end of the month. He'd then attempted to fob him off with a cheque, patently useless as Guzim didn't have a bank account. Guzim had keenly felt the shame of having to repeatedly ask for his dues which the wily English man managed to stiff him on.

I was happy to assure Guzim he would receive cash payments daily. Satisfied with this arrangement Guzim then suggested that he could erect the fence around the stone shed, thus I ended up agreeing I would pay Guzim to put up the fence I was providing at my expense. Returning to the kitchen I wished Spiros a pleasant evening, reflecting that Guzim had somehow managed to get the better of me and most likely wasn't as guileless as he appeared.

Cynthia was full of praise for the remarkable transformation of the house, heaping praise on the work Vangelis had done. Marigold was keen to stress that Barry had played an invaluable part, being able, unlike me, to turn his hand to any practical challenge round the house. Cynthia said she hardly recognised the grand salon, though she had only been in once when she'd helped Spiros' inebriated uncle safely up the stairs.

"A kind gesture I soon regretted because that boorish Harold happened to spot me leaving. I knew just what he was thinking when he saw me, clueless I'd only been in here for two minutes. He's the type to happily besmirch my good reputation amongst the villagers, it's a cross a woman has to bear being single in a small community," Cynthia said.

"I'm sure no one takes any notice of Harold," Marigold reassured her.

"Who would he tell anyway, he can't speak a word of Greek?" I pointed out.

"No, but many of the villagers can understand much more English than they like to let on," Cynthia revealed.

"What did you decide to serve with the fish?" Marigold asked.

"I wonderful medley of colourful and flavoursome Mediterranean vegetables," I replied, remembering I still needed to gut and fillet the fish. Opening the door of Spiros' uncle's massive American refrigerator I was perturbed to see no sign of the fish.

"You did bring it up from the car?" I asked Marigold, clearly recalling she'd said she would bring the fish and fruit up.

"Of course, well I think so; I definitely remember putting the grapes in the fruit bowl," Marigold said evasively, her face riddled with guilt.

The pungent reek of gone-off fish assaulted me when I discovered Marigold had indeed left the fish in the car. The tell-tale grey tint of the slimy coating now enveloping the once healthy looking *lavraki* confirmed my suspicion it had turned in the heat.

"It looks like it is only fit for the cats now, though I'm not sure it's a good idea potentially exposing them to ciguatera or scrombroid poisoning," I hesitated, clueless if cats were susceptible to the same contaminations as people, but wary considering Clawsome's delicate condition.

"Oh you mustn't feed gone off fish to the cats, it could be dangerous," Cynthia said with confidence. "In fact it's never a good idea to treat cats to even fresh fish, not only does it expose them to potentially harmful toxins but they can get far too easily addicted to it. I made the mistake of treating Kouneli to some lovely fresh fish and he ended up totally spoiled, the next time he saw the tin opener he went on hunger strike."

Marigold confirmed with equal confidence that it was always safer to feed cats with specially formulated cat food, a confidence gained from her experience as a pet food taster. Much as I was tempted to sneak the fish to Cynthia's mutant I didn't want to get a reputation as the local cat poisoner.

The *melitzanosalata* I had prepared earlier hardly constituted a meal fit for three people so I suggested adjourning to the local taverna for dinner.

Chapter 27

Pulling the Purse Strings

Nikos was delighted by our return to the taverna, greeting me with another bone crushing handshake. I resolved that I would not allow the filthy state of the place, no cleaner than the last time we visited and still decorated with mosquito laced cobwebs, to deter me from making the most of what promised to be an enjoyable evening. I noticed that Nikos had scraped a razor over his chin stubble since our last visit and that Dina had a Persil white apron tied round her middle.

Dina emerged from the kitchen to smother Cynthia with welcoming hugs, and to hesitantly bestow a couple of shy kisses on Marigold. Vangelis and Athena were seated in the taverna and insisted the three of us join them, telling us we were in for a treat; Nikos had wrung the necks of a couple of chickens that morning. I was happy to note Vangelis was not the type of man to leave his wife stuck at home whilst he frequented the taverna.

I nodded to some of the by now familiar faces, recognising Panos as the Greek bearing grapes, and also Litsa's brother, the elderly man who liked nothing more than piling his bread with slivers of raw garlic. Marigold, obviously recalling Spiros' words about the local barber, discreetly checked out the back of everyone's heads, whispering to me that Spiros was right and everyone did indeed sport a jagged hairline above their necks.

The burden of translating didn't fall entirely on Vangelis' shoulders since Cynthia proved to be quite proficient in the difficult language. In no time at all we were all tucking heartily into bread, salad, and cheese; and grilled chicken topped with fresh oregano served with Dina's marvellous chips. Vangelis clucked his tongue and nodded, the traditional Greek way of voicing disagreement without actually speaking, when I told him I had offered Guzim some work in the garden. His obvious disapproval of my choice of casual garden labourer somewhat dismayed me so I pressed him for the reason.

Vangelis was clear that there was nothing at all wrong with Guzim's actual labour; he was deceptively strong for such a slight man, he followed orders diligently and could turn his hand to most tasks. Nevertheless Vangelis stated he would never again employ Guzim unless he was absolutely desperate. I was curious what Guzim had done to provoke such an uncompromising statement.

"The trouble with Guzim is he pull on the purse strings by working slyly on the heart strings," Vangelis explained. "He tell endlessly all the many troubles, how he is forced to do the menial work in a foreign country with a prejudice against the Albanians, how his poor wife is always destitute and pregnant, as though he had nothing to do with it. We all know hard times, why when Athena and I were first married we too were very poor, or at least not rich in money, but when Athena was pregnant I knew it was my doing and knew responsibility as a man."

"I expect you were never reduced to living in a basic stone shed with an outside hosepipe as a shower though," I commented.

"No, but we not have the privacy the Guzim have in his shed. When we marry we live with my parents, my grandmother, my grandmother's widowed sister, my brother and his wife, and my younger sister, and we all share the one outside bathroom," Vangelis continued, repeating everything in Greek for the benefit of Athena. After listening to something his wife told him he added with a smile, "And Athena say it was not easy at all living with my mother. Did Marigold have to live with the mother of you Victor?"

"No," I stated, without elaborating. My adoptive parents, now sadly deceased, had adored Marigold from the off, treating her as the daughter they never had. Neither Marigold nor I had met my supposed mother, the woman who had abandoned me as a baby in a bucket at the railway station. I contemplated sharing this gem with Vangelis in a game of one-upmanship in the poverty porn stakes, but decided it may all get too much if he wanted to translate the whole sorry saga for Athena's benefit. I was glad in hindsight that I did not raise the matter; it was not a subject suited for the dinner table with new friends.

"So the Guzim tell constantly how poor he is, even though I pay him the going rate. But then he pull on the purse strings, he have no money for the lunch, he say the wife in Albania eat all the money, so I buy him the lunch. Then later he have no the shoe, because the wife in Albania eat all the money and he cannot to afford the new, so I buy him the shoe. Then he cry all the day about the pain in the neck because he has no money to buy the pillow."

"Because the wife in Albania eat all the money," I interrupted.

"Exactly, so I buy him the pillow. Every the day the same, day after day, he has something new to cry on, every day he wear his poorness with no pride, always the tale he have no money because the wife in Albania eat all the money."

"It must have got wearing," I sympathised.

"Yes, but listen Victor, one day I find out he not send the wages to the pregnant wife in Albania at all, he drink all the wages in Amstel. The next time he start the crying he is too poor I got so sick of his whining I gave him the boot. If you give him work you must be heartless Victor, take my advice. He will see you as the rich foreign to exploit."

"Well I've already offered to pay to have a fence erected around his shed and he couldn't have been more grateful," I said, recounting how Guzim had prostrated himself on his knees at the news, with tears running down his face.

"Yes, he is the expert at the tears, be very wary Victor," Vangelis said.

"In fairness the fence is as much for our benefit as his," Marigold said. "I wasn't happy at all about having a bird's eye view of his shed."

"I'll certainly think on what you've said Vangeli," I assured him, having no intention of being taken for the village mug.

Fortunately the subject was changed when Athena started to grill Cynthia about her budding romance with Barry, news of their farewell kiss by the removal van having by now sped allround the village. I felt quite sorry for Cynthia, first subjected to cross-examination by Marigold and now put through the wringer by the inquisitive Athena. Even Vangelis had to put his two-penneth worth in, and if that wasn't enough Panos the grape bearer apparently had to have his say in the matter, followed by Litsa's brother telling Cynthia she'd caught a good one in Barry. Hating to see Cynthia blushing after she had confided she hated to be on the receiving end of gossip, I suggested we take an after dinner constitutional around the plastic chairs on the taverna's outside patio.

"Thank you Victor, it was very thoughtful of you to notice I was embarrassed," she said once we'd made our escape. "I do wish people would keep their noses out of my business. The villagers must already think I'm the local man-eater after Harold stirred the pot with his ridiculous tale of my disgraceful visit to Pedros' place."

"Harold strikes me as the vile bitter type who is no doubt jealous of your obvious popularity amongst the villagers," I said. "You appear to be a very level headed woman and would be a good match for Barry. Oops there I go, sounding just like Marigold."

"It's perfectly fine; I know you meant it in the nicest possible way. It's still very early days with Barry, we only managed to meet a handful of times whilst he was staying with you. Barry is as keen on keeping things private as I am, he knows how curtains can twitch in a small village," Cynthia said.

Bravo Barry, I thought, for managing to keep that little gem from your sister. He had obviously been enjoying secret assignations with Cynthia whilst his sister and I were in town on business, cleverly safeguarding his privacy by telling Marigold that he'd only run into Cynthia once at the shop before he returned the mutant cat.

On our return to the table I was delighted to accept a translated invitation from Panos the grape bearer to call in at his place sometime to check out his grapevine. Athena also extended an invitation for Marigold to join her and some other village ladies who met on the last Friday morning of each month. Marigold promised to put the date in her dairy, no doubt imagining it was a type of coffee morning gathering. To her credit she didn't bat an eyelid when Cynthia translated that she had just been volunteered to help beautify the local cemetery with a spot of weeding.

Vangelis insisted on driving Cynthia home even though it was only a two-minute walk, reminding me as we parted to not allow myself to be duped by Guzim. By the time we left the taverna we felt as though we were beginning to be accepted by the local community.

Chapter 28

Peace and Tranquillity

With a notebook in hand I took a seat on the balcony, having decided to follow Barry's advice and pen an account of our move to Greece. If luck was on my side I would have a few hours before the toxic fumes from Maria's disgusting habit of burning plastic forced me indoors. Whilst I twiddled my pencil, Marigold was busy in the kitchen making fig chutney. I had picked the fruit at first light, feeling a twinge of guilt that I was depriving Guzim of his morning Amstel. Meanwhile Vangelis was hard at work plastering the walls of my would-be office, having declined my offer of help following Barry's sound warning.

Since the balcony overlooked the street I found I was subject to a multitude of distractions whilst I penned my thoughts. Spiros soared by on his bicycle, still helmetless despite his earlier mishap and my subsequent lecture on optimum health and safety guidelines for cyclists. Dina sent me a cheery wave as she walked by on her way to the village shop, piquing my interest in her possible purchase since Nikos professed to grow or kill everything they served. A couple of young children kicking a football around led me to guess one of the villagers was enjoying a visit from the grandchildren, since the village population didn't include any children. I chuckled at the sight of a car speeding by, its roof rack piled high with gaudy beach inflatables. Spotting Harold at the wheel I sighed in relief; if the ghastly pair was off for a day at the beach I wouldn't need to dream up excuses to avoid them.

The enchanting views made the balcony the

perfect setting for relaxing, the various comings and goings below sparking my interest as a keen observer of village habits. I reflected there was nowhere I would rather be than my new home, far away from the pressures of my former daily grind of inspecting restaurant kitchens to ensure they complied with health and safety standards. I recalled Spiros' words the first time he had introduced us to the charms of Meli: "Away from the maddening crowd of tourists you will breathe pure mountain air in the peace and tranquillity," and considered never had words been more apt. Just sitting and absorbing the atmosphere was all I needed to feel contentment, and the air would remain pure until Maria next door set fire to the plastic.

My distracted musings were interrupted by Marigold's hysterical screams. Hoping the goat she'd had the earlier feisty confrontation with hadn't managed to find its way into the kitchen, I rushed in to see what had set her off this time.

"Get it out of here Victor," Marigold cried from her precariously balanced perch on top of the new granite countertop.

"Get what out?" I responded. Vangelis appeared, his face red with alarm, wielding a trowel, presumably planning to use it against whatever had caused my wife to freak out.

"Catastrophe has dragged in a dirty great big lizard," Marigold shouted, pointing to the guilty cat busily tormenting its prey.

"You scream over a lizard?" Vangelis shouted in disbelief.

"It scared the life out of me, what if it gets under the bed. Quick, grab it and get it out of here."

I made an attempt to seize the slinking amphibian, happy to oblige if only to spare it further torture at the paws of the cat. Rushing to catch hold of the lizard I noticed the cat had already succeeded in pulling one of its legs off. Catastrophe had no interest in the scaly foot now littering the kitchen floor, intent on inflicting as much bodily damage as possible on the remaining portion of her prey. Thwarted in her attempts when I gently scooped up the lizard, she sunk her claws into my ankle instead, and then to further express her disapproval proceeded to bite me.

"Marigold, to have the lizard in the house is a sign of the good luck," Vangelis said.

"He's right," I added, wincing in pain. "A

few of these lucky creatures in the bedroom will save us a fortune on anti-mosquito plug-in liquid; they feast on the blood-suckers."

"Over my dead body, I'm not sharing the bedroom with lizards," Marigold retorted. "Do put it outside Victor; it's made me come over all squeamish."

Nodding his head in disbelief Vangelis retreated back to the office, obviously shocked that my wife was not made of sterner stuff. I placed the lizard down gently on the outside stairs, hoping it wouldn't suffer too much from the deleterious effects of losing a leg.

"Don't say a word," Marigold warned me when I re-joined her in the kitchen where she was sealing the lids on a dozen jars of delicious looking chutney, whilst Catastrophe sulked in a corner.

Marigold decided it was now an opportune moment to critique the work I had done on the book, being a self-proclaimed expert in the genre. She wasn't too impressed when she discovered my scribbles only covered a single page since 'I'd been sat on my backside all morning' as she indelicately put it.

"I think you really ought to read some of my

favourite books on the subject of moving abroad to get more of a feel for what readers expect," Marigold said, her nose twitching as she read my words. She advised me that I had neglected to use a suitable number of exclamation marks, a grammatical overkill I considered a slovenly habit. My protestation that I had written nothing that warranted exclamation fell on deaf ears; Marigold was adamant that a generous addition of plings would add a sense of excitement.

"But nothing I've written is exciting," I remonstrated. "It is a simple account of an early retired couple moving countries."

"Then you must liven it up Victor, people look to this kind of thing for inspiration when they fantasise about exchanging their drab lives in England for a dream one in the sunshine, I know I did. Look, here you have written the word sun, but neglected to capitalise it."

"It is grammatically incorrect to capitalise that particular noun mid-sentence," I pointed out.

"But it would make it stand out on the page and make it sound more exciting, especially if you finish each sentence with an exclamation mark. Oh well, it's only your first attempt, you will probably pick up some pointers if you do a bit of reading. I'm only saying if you do it right you could inspire a whole batch of Mancunians to turn into emigrant grecophiles."

Feeling slightly miffed that Marigold was carping on with so much negativity about my first literary endeavour, I was glad when she let the matter drop, turning instead to her plans for ruining my hope for a quiet afternoon.

"Now, we've been so busy ever since we got here that we deserve a bit of relaxation. I thought we could drive down to the coast for a swim and a spot of lunch," Marigold said enthusiastically.

"I was rather looking forward to sampling your chutney with a quiet lunch at home," I said.

My afternoon plans had involved nothing more exacting than another leisurely hour or two on the balcony, before perhaps strolling round to Panos' place to admire his grapevine and practice a few words of my tentative Greek. A drive down to the humid coast, fighting for a free sunbed amidst the tourist throngs, had not been on my afternoon agenda.

"The chutney needs to mature," Marigold

snapped, putting an end to the matter. Marigold pointed out the sea would soon develop a chill as October was almost upon us and we really should make the most of the available bathing window. She said we really should try out a few of the coastal restaurants before they closed down at the end of the tourist season. Reminding her that we'd agreed not to turn into one of those joined-at the-hip couples in retirement, I suggested she go alone. Marigold pulled out her trump card, persuasively reminding me she couldn't possibly handle the left-hand drive car on the bends and we could hardly run to a taxi as I'd blown our entire budget on the new Punto.

Resigned to the inevitable I changed into my swim shorts, wondering if a spot of boot polish would convincingly cover up my greying chest hair or just make me look like a deluded poser.

Chapter 29

No Traditional Features Remaining

The popular seaside village we drove to boasted a beautiful sandy beach, now barely visible through the regimented lines of sunbeds and umbrellas. Cafes and restaurants lined the idyllic seafront, waiters rushing to deliver food and drinks to the tourists taking a break from their sun loungers.

"Imagine what it must have been like in August," I grumbled, trying to find a parking spot, very tempted to go Greek and park on the pavement.

"A nice swim will improve your short temper Victor; I can't think why you can't get in the holiday mood."

"We aren't on holiday," I pointed out, wishing Marigold would stop trying to insist I act like a tourist.

"I'll grab a couple of beds," Marigold volunteered, leaving me to trail across the sand behind her, weighed down with all the unnecessary paraphernalia she'd stuffed into her oversized beach bag. In addition to the sunscreen she'd brought along for a possible top-up despite slathering herself in the stuff before we left home, the bag was overflowing with after-sun cream, a change of outfit to avoid any post-swim dampness, two cumbersome bottles of sparkling water to prevent dehydration, three moving abroad books and enough beach towels to dry an elephant.

Quite why it was necessary to shell out three euros for a couple of sunbeds was beyond me. After dumping our things on the loungers we spent the next hour in the sea and our belongings would have been fine on the beach. The perfect warm embrace of the calm and clear blue water relaxed me; as my mood mellowed I conceded Marigold was right and we should take time out to seize the moment and enjoy the natural delights of our new country. Drifting languidly in the tranquil water of the Messenian Bay, appreciating the magnificent view of the mountain range in the distance capped with blue skies, I reflected it certainly beat a dunking in the Manchester Ship Canal.

Marigold decided a leisurely lunch was in order once we could tear ourselves away from the water. She accepted my apology for my earlier petulance, glowing with pleasure when I paid her the sincere compliment that she looked beautiful with her damp red locks teased by the sea water into natural tendrils. Selecting a shady outside table in a sea-front restaurant we ordered *domates yemistes*, tomatoes stuffed with rice and courgettes. Marigold humoured my preference for a vegetarian option, familiar with my tendency to get twitchy when confronted with meat of possibly dubious origins from an unvetted kitchen.

We had only just relinquished our menus to the waiter when I groaned aloud, unable to conceal my utter dismay when Harold and Joan entered the restaurant, deep in conversation with an innocuous looking middle-aged couple. Abruptly grabbing the menus back from the surprised waiter, we used them as shields to conceal our presence, hoping the ghastly pair wouldn't spot us. Fortunately they passed right by, seemingly oblivious to our presence, taking a seat in the full glare of the sun with their backs to us. The arrival of our freshly squeezed orange juice put paid to my immediate instinct of cancelling our lunch order and legging it at great speed.

"Just try and ignore them, don't let them ruin a nice lunch," Marigold advised, trying to convince herself as much as me that their presence wouldn't put a damper on our mood.

Unfortunately it proved impossible to ignore them; Harold's booming voice reverberating around the restaurant could only be compared to the grating sound of chalk on a blackboard, intrusive and irritating beyond measure, drawing looks of disapproval from the other customers. It was hard to judge from the distance if his companions were red-faced from too much sun or embarrassment. I presumed Harold felt inadequate due to his diminutive stature and overcompensated by talking loudly over everyone. I guessed from his volume that he'd already been on the beer and wondered how he planned to get home. Perhaps in his beer blurred haze he had decided to take his chances and drive under the influence, risking another night in the police cells. Marigold said it was none of our business and with any luck he'd be so sozzled he might drive over the cliff edge.

Determined not to let Harold spoil our lunch we tucked into the *domates yemistes* with relish, unwilling to invite indigestion by rushing our food. As Harold's words washed over us we started to laugh contagiously, his words so outrageous that we couldn't believe our ears. He was apparently holding court over a pair of captive tourists he was desperate to impress with exaggerated boasts about his wonderful life in Greece.

"He's changed his tune," I said to Marigold as we settled back to eavesdrop on his fabricated tales about his fabulous fantasy life that bore no relation to the reality he'd painted when he'd first intruded on us in Meli. I decided to pay attention to the undiluted garbage spewing from his mouth, knowing Vangelis and Cynthia would both get a kick out of the re-telling.

"You'll love it, we do, never regretted the move for a minute. If we didn't have to move back to old Blighty on account of Joan's mother catching dementia and getting all forgetful you wouldn't be able to drag us away," Harold lied.

"It seems such a shame that you have to give up your dream home in the sun, especially as you said you've had so much work done to make it just perfect," the woman they were with said sympathetically.

"It fair breaks our hearts, doesn't it Joan, so much money and time spent doing it up. Of course we could see the potential of the old place from the off; it just needed a heck of a lot of work doing to drag it into the twenty-first century, but now we've knocked it into top-notch shape. The locals couldn't believe what we were having done to the place, but they seem happy enough to muck along living like peas-ants, stuck in the rut of their old time ways. I al-ways say if we Brits had lost the war to the Greeks we'd still be mucking along with outside lavvies, don't I Joan?"

"Oh you do Harold, he's always saying if the Greeks had won the war and invaded England we'd all still be living in two-up two-down back-to-backs with outside lavvies," Joan confirmed.

"With goats and cockerels having free run of the back yard."

I almost choked on my mouthful of tomato in my attempt to cover the involuntary snort that escaped me. Not only were Harold and Joan vulgar in the extreme, but their confusion over historical events revealed they were as thick as the proverbial two short planks.

"When we first bought the old place it had those little pokey windows with wooden shutters, but we soon got rid and had them replaced with huge picture windows. Then there was them horrible floor tiles that had been there since the place was built, can you imagine old and cold tiles with no under-floor heating to warm our tootsies? Course they had to go, so we had them ripped out and had thick shag-pile carpets laid wall–to-wall in every room. Course we had to have them shipped out from England, you just can't get quality nylon carpets over here," Harold pontificated, proving he was not only thick and vulgar, but unappreciative of traditional features that were there for a reason.

BUCKET TO GREECE

The traditional old village houses in Meli had been architecturally designed to be cool in summer and warm in winter; the latticed shutters welcoming in Mediterranean breezes often preceded the advent of glass in the windows. The mosaic tiled floors were influenced by classic style dating back to ancient Greece, again perfect for keeping houses cool during the long hot summers. I shuddered at the changes Harold had inflicted on his traditional house. The large picture windows would make the place as hot as a furnace in summer and the nylon shag-pile carpets would trap the heat inexorably. I pondered if perhaps the heat had gone to Harold's head, addling his brain.

"Anyway you'll see for yourself later, we'll head up there after a gyros platter and a bit of lubrication," Harold continued. "You won't be disappointed, we've had it done up a treat. We had a lovely new kitchen we shipped out from Blighty put in, and a bath big enough for the two of us to splash round in together."

His last comment elicited a sharp nudge from Marigold. She could barely suppress her laughter at the thought of the two tubs of lard squeezing into a bath together, the water no doubt splashing over the sides to soak into the nylon shag-pile. Harold's monotonous boasting continued to dominate the restaurant as he turned to his favourite subject.

"Of course we have the best swimming pool for miles, everyone is green with envy. People are always wanting to come and see it, aren't they Joan?"

"Oh yes, we can't keep our fellow Brits in the village away, there's nothing goes down better than a barbecue round at ours and a dip in the pool. We've had some marvellous pool parties, haven't we Harold," Joan wittered.

The couple they were with finally managed to get a word in, saying they were concerned about water shortages in the high mountain village and worried that if they opted for a house with a pool they may be exacerbating the water situation.

"You don't have to worry about that," Harold boomed. "There's plenty of water round here, look, there's even a sea full of the stuff. And we've found a neat little trick to keep the water bill down by topping the pool up with water from the free taps in this village. We fill up a few containers when we come down to the beach, don't we Joan?"

"I thought those taps provided fresh drinking water from mountain springs," their male companion said.

"They do, but there's no law saying you can't swim in it," Harold chortled.

"We did worry the property might be a bit too isolated for us, but it's a relief to hear there are other Brits in the village who've made the move," Harold's male companion continued. "And what about the Greeks in the village, are they quite accepting of foreigners?"

"Couldn't be a nicer lot, could they Joan, always stopping for a chat or popping round to admire the pool."

"Lovely people," Joan concurred.

"That's good to hear, we didn't know how they'd feel about foreigners moving in so it's a relief to hear how friendly they are, and of course if they stop for a chat there mustn't be any language issues."

"Oh we get by, if you can manage the basic of beera and just stick a kali in front of everything you say then you won't go far wrong," Harold said, adding, "Course the Greeks try to speak a bit of English because we bring the money in. They do like our money, I'm always saying to Joan that us Brits moving over here is a big boon to the local economy, why we must spend a fortune in the village shop on beer."

"You do Harold," Joan concurred.

"It would appear Harold is schmoozing some potential house buyers," I whispered to Marigold. "With any luck they'll buy it, thus ridding the village of that vulgar pair."

"I thought it a bit unlikely they actually had any friends," Marigold laughed. "Let's hope they take the bait, though it may prove difficult to sell a traditional Greek house that has had all the traditional features ripped out."

Just then the waiter who was hurrying to deliver drinks to tourists on the sunbeds littering the beach had the misfortune to trip over a stray cat that was hanging round desperate for scraps. His tray went flying in the air, the resounding crash of broken glass attracting everyone's attention. As Harold swivelled his head to gawp at the free entertainment he caught sight of us, by now openly engrossed in our eavesdropping, a look of confusion fleetingly etched on his face. I broke his stare by leaping forward to stop the young waiter from picking the broken glass up by hand, a clear violation of the health and safety protocol for hospitality workers when dealing with dangerous shards. Only when the waiter had been safely persuaded to sweep up the glass with a broom and keep his hands well out of it, did I resume my seat, hoping that Harold may have forgotten we were there as I paid the bill.

My hopes of a discreet exit were in vain. As soon as we stood up to leave Harold shouted loudly, "Here Vic, over here, come over and say hello."

"Play nice, we want him to sell up," Marigold whispered. "It could put the potential buyers off if they sense our disgust."

"I shall make out we are bosom pals if it helps to rid the village of them," I agreed, plastering a fake smile on my face as we approached Harold and his captive companions.

Harold jumped to his feet to greet us bombastically. Either he was a brilliant actor putting on an Oscar worthy performance of false friendship, or he had completely forgotten all about the ignominious bacon incident and genuinely confused me as someone who had time for him.

"Tony, Tess, meet Vic and Marigold, our fellow Brits who live up in Meli and are great friends of ours, great friends aren't they Joan," Harold introduced us. Tony and Tess smiled a little warily; most likely suspicious that any great friends of Harold may prove to be as obnoxious as him.

"Tony and Tess are thinking of buying our place and moving over here."

"I'd be keen to hear your thoughts on living in a high-up mountain village," Tony said. "We're a bit in two minds between the mountains and the coast."

"They're new to the place so won't be able to tell you anything useful," Harold interrupted before we could answer. "Anything you need to know just ask me, me and Joan have been out here for three years you know, not like this pair of newbies. They haven't had time to get their feet wet yet."

I could feel my fake smile beginning to crack under Harold's superior dismissal of our opinion as being of no value due to our greenness. Only the feel of Marigold's hand squeezing my own in warning prevented me from blurting out that Harold would have nothing of value to impart due to his sheer ignorance. Harold, determined I wouldn't be allowed to get a word in edgeways, effectively stage managed our exit by shouting, "Now then Vic, it's pool time at ours tomorrow, don't forget, and don't forget to bring a few bottles to wash down the barbecue. Come over in your cossies, no need to stand on ceremony."

His last dig was no doubt aimed at the long trousers I had changed into after my swim, feeling it totally inappropriate to frequent a restaurant in swimwear, a standard obviously not shared by Harold who found nothing amiss about sitting around in a pair of wet budgie smugglers.

"Ah yes, one of your famous pool parties Harold," I replied with a diplomatic nod which Harold could choose to interpret as acceptance of his invitation or agreement that his pool parties were indeed famous, I really couldn't care less. I had no intention of partying with the uncouth couple or of popping round to feed his vanity by admiring his pool. I felt I had gone above and beyond by biting my tongue and avoiding a scene in front of the nice tourist couple held captive by Harold.

Chapter 30

An Invitation into Guzim's Shed

Marigold admitted on the drive back to the house that she would quite enjoy a peek inside Harold's house, sure that the interior design horrors he'd subjected it to must be far more hideous than anything she could imagine. I finally agreed that if Harold persisted in insisting we pop round to admire his pool that it may be easier to just get it over with, for a quiet life. Our aim was to sever the relationship Harold hoped to establish, being seemingly too thick-skinned to take a hint. We decided that rather than avoiding him we would accept the next invitation to admire his pool. I would then monopolise the conversation by talking down to him, literally as I tower over him from my superior height, volubly mock every tasteless change he had made to his traditional residence and bore him rigid with self-righteous indignation about his irresponsible wastage of water, citing endless tedious statistics.

"It's perfect Victor." Marigold trilled. "One of your monotonous and pompous lectures is guaranteed to ensure we are never invited back again, you've really no idea how boring you can be when you get your teeth stuck into a dull subject."

"Well I will deliberately drone on to achieve our purpose," I pointed out, slightly miffed how readily my wife agreed I could be boring.

It was late afternoon by the time we arrived back in Meli. I felt a tad guilty when I discovered Guzim had already made a start on the garden since I'd neglected to take any garden implements out of the ground floor storage for his convenience. The Albanian had worked up a powerful sweat pulling reluctant weeds out by hand, fighting to yank out roots baked solidly in place. The garden covered such a large area that it would be a monumental job to get the whole thing cleared and although Guzim and the borrowed goat had made a sterling start it only made a dent in the overgrown wilderness. Of course I intended to get stuck in too and made a mental note to purchase a petrol strimmer in town, confident it wouldn't prove too difficult to get the hang of.

I was gratified to notice Guzim had started by clearing an area closest to the house which Marigold had plans to turn into an herb garden. I had sketched out a few plans on paper depicting the ideal placement for the herb garden and vegetable patches, and once the weeds were vanquished I intended to establish a few paths to give easy access to the fruit trees. Whilst Guzim tackled his weedy patch I grabbed a pencil and paper, deciding I would finally take a full inventory of the fruit trees we had. Spiros had already pointed out that I was now the proud owner of a magnificent old olive tree producing wonderful eating olives; I would practice my

Greek by bending the ear of the locals about the best way to cure and preserve them, Panos was sure to have a few tips worth sharing from his years of experience.

In addition to the olive and fig trees, the garden hosted a selection of orange, lemon and nectarines trees. To my surprise I also discovered a couple of pomegranate trees, their branches already weighed down with ripening fruit. Their discovery was such a wonderful find that I determined to change my priorities and make the garden the first order of business for the foreseeable. I would dedicate a few hours each morning before the heat of the sun made the work too onerous. Together with Guzim's contribution, the jungle could be transformed into a pleasant and produce rich garden. Stepping warily through the undergrowth in case any snakes lurked, I chanced upon a caper shrub, happy to think how much it would please Marigold; she had a particular addiction for the piquant buds.

Raiding the storage I found an old trowel and hoe to present to Guzim for future work. He was glad of the chance for a break, demonstrating with weary gestures and groans that it was back-breaking work. In turn I indicated by pointing to my watch that it was time to call it a day, handing over a crisp ten euro note as per our agreement. I was surprised when Guzim indicated that I should follow him into his shed; he obviously wanted to show off the old homestead when he repeated the words *"ela spiti mou."* The small space was crammed with a single iron bedstead piled high with a collection of rather odorous old blankets that bore a remarkable resemblance to the ones Spiros' uncle had bedded down under; I surmised Guzim may have retrieved his disgusting bedding from the tip.

An old fridge was pushed next to the bed, its unsteady vibrations causing the gas camping stove balanced on top to wobble precariously. Tempted as I was to warn Guzim of the potential fire hazard the camping stove presented, I lacked the Greek words to press the point. The dented stainless steel sink the kitchen man had tried to palm off on Marigold languished on the floor of the shed; not plumbed in it served as a receptacle for Guzim's many empty Amstel bottles. As a finishing touch Guzim's holey socks dripped from a washing line draped across the room.

BUCKET TO GREECE

The whole miserable set up gave me an immediate sense of déjà vu and I racked my brain to try to fathom why it felt so familiar. Images of a rather shabby restaurant I had once inspected flooded my mind. The grouchy owner had reluctantly shown me around, annoyed when I insisted on inspecting a shed in the back yard. Complaining there was nothing to see in there but a spare fridge, he swore under his breath when I insisted on seeing for myself. Inside the shed one of his members of staff was using the vibrating fridge as a table for her lunch. Bizarrely she was seated beneath what appeared to be that day's takings, a row of one pound notes pegged to a washing line flapping above her head. I wondered if this strange method of dealing with the takings rather than keeping them in a cash register had anything to do with money laundering, but since the restaurant's finances were not within my specified remit I didn't comment. The shed as a makeshift dining room didn't appear to violate any health regulations I could think of, being clean if nothing else. As we left the shed I apologised to the young waitress for disturbing her lunch break and asked if she was enjoying the food.

"It's not too bad once you get used to faggots, it's all the old skinflint ever dishes up for the staff," she replied.

I surmised Guzim's dripping socks were a special touch he'd laid on for my benefit since it made no sense to have them drip-dry over his blankets rather than outside in the sunshine. I guessed he had carefully orchestrated the scene to play up his poverty when he began to point at his shoes, showing me the sole hanging loose and muttering *"papoutsia"* and *"trypa."* Although I hadn't yet come across these words in the archaic phrase book it wasn't a leap to suppose they meant shoes and hole. Recalling Vangelis' warning that Guzim would attempt to play on my heart strings to pull at my purse strings I pulled out a phrase I had practiced for this exact eventuality, saying *"sas ethosa lefta,"* meaning "I gave you money."

Guzim followed me back outside, pulling one shoe off to wave the flapping sole under my nose. I won't deny that the gesture did indeed pull at my heartstrings as I reflected I was rich in material things while in contrast Guzim had so little. Nevertheless I recognised Guzim was guilty of attempting to manipulate me by inviting me into his home, a home that according to Vangelis would not be such a slum if Guzim didn't drink all his wages. I recalled he had just earned a day's wages though labouring, an amount supplemented by the ten euros I'd then handed over for his work in the garden.

Gesturing that Guzim should wait there and I would return, I spotted a sly look come over his face: I interpreted it as him thinking he had successfully played me, probably expecting me to return bearing a gift of shoes from my own wardrobe. Striding back to the house with a hardened heart I speculated how Guzim had managed to save up enough money to purchase the shed from Spiros' uncle since he drank all his wages, and made a mental note to find out from Spiros how much Guzim had paid for the shed.

Guzim looked decidedly smug when I re-turned, no doubt congratulating himself on how easy it had been to fleece the gullible foreigner. However I had not taken Vangelis' advice lightly and Guzim was the one taken completely aback when I presented him with a piece of sturdy cardboard to stuff into his shoe. Spitting contemptuously into the weeds, he took the cardboard and stuffed it into his shoe resignedly, before completely surprising me by proffering a warm bottle of Amstel.

Chapter 31

A Burke from the Blue

Marigold and I spent the evening relaxing with a glass of wine on the roof terrace. The nights had begun to draw in and we let the darkness envelop us, only the flickering wicks of the citronella candles casting light into the shadows. The temperature dropped after sunset, a relief after the heat of the day; the silence only broken by the persistent hoot of an owl and the muted conversation of villagers passing by on the street.

V.D. BUCKET

We spoke in hushed tones of our plans for the future. Marigold was keen to visit a few garden centres for inspiration and had unearthed a long forgotten gardener's almanac with handy tips on monthly planting. Keen to expand her circle of friends, she planned to introduce herself to the other foreign residents of Meli, and was quite looking forward to meeting up with the Greek ladies for her rendezvous in the cemetery. I shared my own plans to dedicate a few hours each morning to tackling the garden; my determination to master a petrol strimmer, to arrange some Greek lessons, pen a few words of the book and drop in on Panos and his grapevine.

A definite chill in the air roused Marigold and she disappeared downstairs in search of a cardigan. The drop in temperature reminded me I must source some logs for the fireplace. Though for now we could make the most of our evenings outside, I expected that in a couple of months we would be curled up inside in front of a blazing fire. My musings were interrupted by the sound of Marigold calling my name; I hoped Catastrophe hadn't dragged another lizard indoors to torment.

BUCKET TO GREECE

When I entered the house Marigold beckoned, her hand covering up the telephone receiver as she told me Gary from Manchester was on the line insisting it was urgent and I should hurry as he'd taken the liberty of reversing the charges.

"Gary?" I asked, perplexed. The only Gary I knew was a chef currently serving six years in Strangeways for poisoning a room full of guests at a wedding reception, but that may explain the collect call. I'd considered his arrest most harsh since he claimed the mass poisoning was accidental and he'd no idea the savoury mousse in the bain-marie had been contaminated with Escherichia coli. I had been called as a defence witness at the time of his trial to testify Gary had always kept a pristine kitchen. He later confessed his guilt, admitting in a moment of passionate jealousy he had deliberately served up contaminated food when he realised the bride was his ex. To be fair he had only intended to poison the groom and the other fifty near fatalities were completely incidental. Still, I couldn't imagine why he was calling me now, unless he hadn't heard I'd retired and wanted me to inspect the prison kitchen.

Taking the phone from Marigold I tentatively asked, "Gary, how's prison treating you?"

"What mate? This is Gary what bought your house in Manchester; I've never been in the big house. I got your number off the estate agent, he was that reluctant to hand it over, but I prised it out of him 'cos it's urgent."

It transpired the culinary troglodyte builder buyer actually had a name, but that didn't explain why he was calling long distance and reversing the charges.

"Is there a problem with the house?" I asked in concern.

"No, nothing like that mate, in fact it turned out it didn't need a new roof after all, saved me a fortune," Gary revealed. "No, I'm calling about this batty old woman what I can't get shot off, a right old battle- axe she is too. She turned up a week ago claiming to be my mother, a right fruit cake she is; imagine the notion that I wouldn't know my own mother. I sent her packing, but she was back the next day, refusing to budge from the porch, going on till she was blue in the face that she knew damn well I was her son and she wouldn't be told otherwise unless I could prove I wasn't with a DNA test. Batty she is, have you seen the price of them DNA tests? I nearly called the plod thinking she had dementia and had wandered off from somewhere."

"I fail to see what any of this has to do with me Gary," I interrupted.

"Well here's the thing, she turned up again today claiming this was definitely the address the Salvation Army had traced her long lost son to. I insisted she was no relation of mine, but when she kept going on about the address I thought she must be something to do with you, even though she claimed her son was called Victor. In the end she wore me down and I gave her your new address in Greece. I knew it was a stupid thing to do, but I was that desperate to get rid of her and she kept threatening to handbag me. Anyway the wife give me a right telling off, saying I'd best warn you the mad old hag is planning to turn up on your doorstep in Greece, I could kick myself for lumbering you with her, especially when she's after someone called Victor Donald and that's not even your name. It was her going on about the address that confused me, but I shouldn't have dragged you into it."

"I'm sorry, I have to go," I said, dropping

the phone and slumping onto my haunches.

Of course Gary hadn't realised my name was Victor Donald since I had never used the name safety pinned to the pink frilly bonnet I was found in. I was only ever Victor for the briefest of time, being fortunate enough to have been adopted and name changed very quickly. There had supposedly been a veritable glut of sympathetic do-gooders eager to adopt me when word that a baby had been abandoned in a bucket at the railway station got out, it being the sort of sad story to tear at the public heart-strings, especially in the Christmas season with the end of the war imminent. The irony wasn't lost on me that I was about to dust off the name of Victor Bucket to use as my literary pseudo-nym, but until now the name had lain dormant for fifty-eight years.

And now it appeared the woman who had abandoned me in a bucket without even demon-strating enough sense of basic hygiene to scrub it clean of coal dust, was making a nuisance of herself on my old doorstep after keeping silent for almost six decades.

In truth I hadn't wasted much more than a passing thought on my absconded parent in years. My adoptive parents had never attempted to conceal the truth from me, but I had no interest in delving into my murky beginnings, notable only by a pink frilly bonnet and soot stained coal bucket. I can't really explain why I still carry a faded cutting from the Manchester Evening News in my wallet. Even though I'd made the headlines, the police turned up no leads regarding my birth mother, and as for a possible father, it was pointless to speculate.

It was only when Barry was born six months after my wedding to Marigold that I became curious about the woman who had abandoned me. The birth of a child raised all kinds of questions about possibly dodgy family medical histories that I was unable to answer and suddenly wanted answers to. My search proved fruitless, even the brightest brains in the Salvation Army unable to turn up a lead. Eventually, after several years of searching, I gave up; it was futile to search for someone who had no desire to be found. After the passage of so much time I preferred to presume the absconded parent was dead and buried, and I conveniently suppressed any fleeting thoughts on the matter.

Now, with one phone call, my equanimity was shattered, a thousand questions buzzing in my head. I thought back to what Gary had said but his words only gave his impression: an impression of a batty old battle-axe who was as mad as a fruit cake, but determined, very determined to find her long lost son. Whether I chose to be found had been taken out of my hands since Gary had impetuously provided her with my Greek address.

"What on earth are you doing slumped on the floor?" Marigold asked. "Why didn't you come back to the terrace, I've been missing you?"

Not sure what to say, I simply shrugged.

"Oh, don't start going all Greek on me, whatever has happened? Is it something to do with that phone call?"

As Marigold helped me to my feet I said, "I think we'll need a drink."

Returning to the roof terrace with a newly opened bottle of Metaxa, I recounted Gary's phone call to my wife. She was as shell shocked as I but took a more practical approach, saying we must get to the bottom of it, pointing out Gary had mentioned she'd been almost a permanent fixture on his porch and he must have more details.

"Let me see to it dear, I'll ring our old number and find out as much as I can; here have a top up and try not to stress out," Marigold said.

Lost in my thoughts I had no idea how long Marigold was gone, but the bottle of brandy was half-empty by the time she returned. Taking my hand she said, "Her name is Violet Burke."

"So it turns out that I am not a bucket but I am a burke," I said dolefully.

"Not necessarily Victor, Burke may be her married name."

"Tell me the worst, I've a feeling I'm not going to like what I hear," I said, not expecting this Burke woman to have transformed from a batty old battle-axe into a respectable grandmother for Benjamin in the space of one phone call.

"Well according to Gary whom we sold the house to she first turned up a week ago. He opened the door only to be nearly smothered with unwelcome hugs. He was very naturally confused by a woman proclaiming to be his mother, especially since his own mother was enjoying a week's break in Blackpool, taking in the Illuminations. When he refused to accept this complete stranger was his mother she started ranting about how she should have known he'd be ashamed of her and want nothing to do with her."

"Did he mention what she looked like?" I asked, barely daring to exhale.

"I knew you'd want to know so I pressed him for a description, I'm afraid it wasn't very flattering. He said she was a bit blowsy, mutton dressed-like-lamb and a bit heavy handed with the make-up, with badly dyed red hair," Marigold reluctantly added, painfully aware the colour of her own once Titan hair now came out of a bottle.

"Don't even think about putting some Freudian interpretation on that," I said, putting a comforting arm around Marigold, aware she would be adding some psychoanalytic twist to the coincidence of my decamped mother and wife both being redheads. "I had no idea my birth mother had red hair and for all we know this Violet person may never have been a redhead, but simply enjoys experimenting with colour. Tell me more of what you learned from Gary."

"The first time she turned up he just thought

she was a bit loopy and sent her packing. Then she became more persistent, refusing to budge from the porch until he admitted he was her son, which he naturally refused to do. This morning she was back again, and when she told him his address had been traced through the Salvation Army he explained he'd only very recently moved into the property. When she still refused to listen, insisting she had rights and again demanding he take a DNA test, he handed over our new address just to get rid of her," Marigold recounted, pausing suddenly. "You know Victor we have both jumped to what appears to be an obvious conclusion, but there's not actually a scrap of evidence that this Violet Burke person is your long lost mother, she could be an imposter. If by any chance she does find you it is you who should demand a DNA test."

"But she was looking for Victor," I pointed out.

"And that name was printed in the newspapers at the time. She could be some grasping old gold digger looking for a comfortable billet to see out her old age," Marigold reasoned.

"No, I feel it in my gut, this is no imposter," I stated.

"Well unfortunately Gary could provide no other details beyond her name. He was hardly likely to ask for the address and telephone number of someone he was desperate to be rid of. He didn't disclose our telephone number; he only got it out of the estate agent this evening," Marigold said.

"So we are sitting ducks, waiting for this Violet Burke to turn up unannounced at any moment," I said flatly, taking another large slug of Metaxa.

"Victor, she's hardly likely to turn up tomorrow, think about it, she's an old age pensioner. For all you know she's never been abroad and will be clueless how to find her way to Meli. It's a long way to come on the off-chance, not to mention expensive."

"Oh she'll come; I feel it in my gut."

"And how do you feel about it, it's such a shock?"

"I don't know," I answered truthfully. It was all such a bolt from the blue, or rather a burke from the blue.

Chapter 32

Dousing the Fire

In the days following Gary's phone call about the sudden unexpected appearance of Violet Burke, I must confess to falling into a morose slump, most uncharacteristic of my usually equanimity. Marigold, whilst sympathetic to the shock I'd received, was beginning to get fed up with, as she put it, "you moping about the place." She insisted we drive up to town to purchase the petrol strimmer I had mentioned; telling me that weed-whacking would be excellent therapy, allowing me to take my frustrations out on something that deserved cutting down to size. I suspected another ulterior motive; Marigold presumed I was so consumed by my inner turmoil that I might not notice if she was a bit free with the credit card. I did notice her rather reckless spending on scatter cushions and Greek vases, but chose to say nothing; after all she deserved a bit of a spree for putting up with my intolerable mood.

Donning an old motorcycle helmet and goggles that Vangelis had kindly lent me for protection when strimming, I headed into the garden to grapple with the new petrol-powered tool. As Marigold had guessed, a spot of weed-whacking proved to be very cathartic; I imagined the weeds as a monstrous image of a gargantuan Violet Burke topped with a bulbous red head. Even though my conjured image had no features it felt satisfying to swing the strimmer mercilessly as though I was a latter-day Don Quixote tilting at windmills. My phantom image of Violet Burke was suddenly enveloped in clouds of noxious smoke and I threw the strimmer down in irritation, almost taking my foot off in the process. Having mentally slayed the phantom of Violet Burke it was now time to stand up to the old woman next door and put an end to her vile and disgusting habit of burning plastic.

Grabbing the length of hosepipe coiled up outside Guzim's stone shed, I hoisted myself onto the garden wall separating my land from that of Kyria Maria, directing the full force of the water towards Maria's garden bonfire. Unfortunately my aim was askew and my grand gesture of defiance ended up soaking Maria before quenching the fire. My elderly neighbour understandably screamed when the shock of cold water hit her. The water fizzled out, Marigold having rushed to turn off the tap when she caught sight of what I was up to. The cessation of water did nothing to stop Maria's hysterical screams; it was only when Marigold bodily shook me and pointed to my goggles and helmet that I understood my appearance must seem disturbingly threatening to my pensioner neighbour.

Maria's cries brought Vangelis running to her assistance, clearing the wall in one fell swoop to gain access to her garden. Removing the goggles and helmet to reveal my identity caused Maria to stare at me incredulously, shouting "Victor, *yiati, yiati*?"

"She wants to know why you tried to drown her," Victor said.

"I didn't, I was aiming the water at her blasted bonfire," I explained.

"Victor's aim has never been good," Marigold interjected. "He always was useless when he played catch with Benjamin."

"Please express my sincere apologies to Kyria Maria for soaking her. In my defence the rancid smoke from her fire nearly blinded me and I almost did myself an injury with the strimmer," I said.

"It really was a mistake letting you loose with a power tool Victor; I should have listened to Barry, he warned me you were a danger to yourself with anything sharper than a butter knife when you've no coordination at all. Look how closely you came to losing a foot," Marigold said.

Looking down I nearly passed out in fright when I saw I'd somehow managed to strim the toes of my work boots clean off. Luckily I had borrowed them from Vangelis, along with the goggles and helmet, and they happened to be a good six inches too big for my feet.

Consoling the still shaking Maria, Vangelis let rip. "You could have given her the heart attack Victor. Imagine the terror when she saw a hosepipe wielding assailant with the face and head covered like the common bank robber."

"Well in Victor's defence he does look more stupid than terrifying in that strimming get-up," Marigold interjected. "And we're all at our wits end with the constant burning. Think of poor pregnant Clawsome forced to inhale that toxic smoke; I wouldn't be at all surprised if it results in the birth of a litter of mutants."

"It would be difficult to establish the toxic smoke as the definitive cause of any mutation if the father is indeed unmasked as Cynthia's grotesque aberration of a rabbit cat," I pointed out, receiving a withering look from Marigold for my pedantry.

"*Ti, Ti?*" Maria cried, demanding to know what was being said. Vangelis and Maria engaged in what appeared to be a heated argument. It was impossible for me to make head or tail of their rapid-fire Greek punctuated with wild gesticulations, only ending when Maria flounced off into her house and Vangelis vaulted back over the wall, announcing he was going to unlock the new gate.

"Why?" I asked.

"Because you have invited the Maria into the home to discuss the matter of the burning plastic in the amicable manner. I tell you I not want to be involved in this possible feud, but it can perhaps be sorted with a little tact and the diplomacy. Maria very much to like you as the neighbour and not to realise the smoke would make you act crazy," Vangelis responded.

Ten minutes later Maria was installed in our kitchen nursing a cup of strong Greek coffee. Clucking her approval at our choice of new units, she ran her soot stained fingers across the brand new granite countertop, before dissolving into tears she proceeded to dab with an enormous handkerchief, apparently overcome with the beauty of the ceramic Butler sink, the like of which she had never seen before. Adopting a stiff upper lip, I simultaneously bit my tongue when Maria freely opened our cupboard doors, exclaiming in wonder as she examined my secret stash of Fray Bentos pies. With no regard to hygiene she stuck a finger into a jar of Marmite, wincing with disgust as she licked the finger clean. I made a mental note to chuck the offending jar into the rubbish and rushed to put the solitary bottle of Heinz salad cream out of her reach before she could violate it in a similar way. Before I could stop Maria her soot stained fingers were making random prods inside jars of chilli powder and bottles of minced ginger, rendering them unfit for cooking and only fit for the bin. I reflected that although her interest was no doubt piqued by these foreign curiosities, that was no excuse for her insanitary finger poking frenzy.

Vangelis finally persuaded Maria to take a seat, allowing her to speak at length before translating for our benefit. He told us that she had caught Spiros' uncle, Pedros, rummaging through the bins over twenty years ago when they first became an eyesore in the village. Denouncing him as a thieving gypsy, he retaliated by calling her names no decent woman would ever repeat, resulting in the two of them almost coming to blows in the street. Maria decided that even the rubbish was not safe from prying eyes in a village where everyone stuck their nose into everyone else's business, and vowed to burn it in future. The resultant smoke drove

Pedros ballistic, an unexpected benefit in Maria's eyes since she derived enormous enjoyment from tormenting her neighbour. The more Pedros implored her to stop, the more she determined to continue, even scavenging extra plastic rubbish from the bins to bring home and burn. She vowed to burn her rubbish every day until the foul practice forced him to move or killed him off, revelling in winding Pedros up.

"She say she has the irrepressibly mischievous nature," Vangelis said.

"She considers pyromania resulting in excessive pollution to be nothing more than an act of mischief?" I snorted. "The Greek law must be lax to let her get away with it for so long."

"Maria say since the Pedros fell off the roof and make the mess on the pavement, she has not the reason to burn the rubbish, but it has become the habit," Vangelis said, sighing over the petty feud that lasted for two decades.

"Spiros never mentioned he fell off the roof," I said, puzzled that he would neglect to mention this detail.

My words were drowned out by Harold calling up loudly from the street. The new lockable gate prevented him from simply barging in so he had resorted to bellowing from the street at full volume to attract our attention. "I'll go down and try to get rid of him," Marigold offered.

Turning to Vangelis I suggested, "As Maria admits she only continues to burn out of habit, perhaps she would now consider stopping, in the name of good neighbourly relations."

"Maria say she think you could be the good neighbour, but is not sure. I am sorry to say this Victor but she worry you may turn into the arrogant foreigner who throw the party without inviting her."

"But we haven't thrown any parties," I protested. "The only thing remotely party like on our agenda is Spiros' idea of having the priest round to bless the house when all the work is finished. Of course we will invite Maria to attend the blessing."

"But she say, would you to invite her to the pool party?"

"Well no, it may have escaped her notice but the nearest thing we have to a swimming pool is the puddle left by Guzim's leaking hose-pipe."

"Maria say the other foreigns are always

having the pool party but because she is old and not British they ignore her. It pains her to feel excluded in her own village where she has lived for eighty years."

Vangelis' words created instant conflict in my mind. I felt for Maria, old and feeling excluded, but reasoned if her behaviour with our Marmite and spices was any indication of how she generally carried on in other people's houses it was hardly surprising she was kept at a distance. A germ of a scheme sprouted in my brain as I suddenly conceived an idea that would make Maria feel included in foreign goings on in the village and would at the same time put an end to Harold harassing us to attend his pool parties.

"Vangelis, tell Maria that if she promises to never burn plastic again, then she will go to a pool party. In fact I'm sure Marigold would be delighted to lend her one of her costumes. I'll be back in a moment."

Rushing downstairs I attempted to interrupt Harold's droning spiel about how the potential buyers he'd been lunching with had turned out to be dreadful time wasters who had failed to put an offer in on his property. Turning to me he said, "They were downright rude about our purple shag-pile. Anyway enough about them, when are you two coming to a pool party, just say the word."

"We'll be delighted to pop over in, let's see, shall we say, thirty minutes? It will be all right with you if we bring a friend along."

"The more the merrier," Harold shouted enthusiastically, unable to believe he was finally going to have the opportunity to impress us with his superior house. As he rushed off to put the beer on ice and fire up the barbecue Marigold looked at me worriedly, saying, "Victor, are you sure about this. I know we discussed going over to ridicule the place and bore him so much he would beg us never to darken his door again, but the mood you've been in lately I thought you'd gone off the idea."

"It will be just the tonic I need," I assured her.

"And who is this mysterious friend we'll be taking along?" Marigold asked, the twinkle in her eye revealing she knew I was up to some mischief.

"Well Kyria Maria is so desperate to be included in a pool party that we will take her along on the promise that she will cease the filthy habit of burning plastic. You don't mind lending her one of your swimming costumes, do you dear?"

"Oh Victor, it will be worth it to see Harold's face when we turn up with a Greek guest, you know how he simply abhors the thought of mixing with the locals."

"I'll be sure to ask Vangelis to translate that she must feel free to stick her fingers into everything she can get her hands on," I laughed.

Chapter 33

Taking the Plunge

In spite of my most persuasive tactics Vangelis had flatly refused to join us, saying life was too short to mix with that oik, leaving Marigold and I to accompany Kyria Maria to her first ever foreign pool party. Without Vangelis along to translate I was forced to resort to a recitation of my well-rehearsed stock of archaic Greek phrases to communicate with Maria as we made our way there. She duly sympathised when she heard a sheep had eaten my last sandwich, but spat contemptuously in the street when I said her prime minister was very handsome. Managing to pick out the odd word from the stream of invective she fired off in response to my phrase, I gathered that Maria was a lifelong member of the Communist Party and despised New Democracy.

To say that Harold was perturbed when we arrived with the eighty-year-old Greek woman in tow decked out in Marigold's most unflattering swimming costume, was an understatement. I knew from the way he'd considered Barry to be beneath contempt, not even worthy of greeting when he mistook him for a foreign workman, and from the way in which he'd declared Cynthia to be a loose hussy for fraternising with a supposedly foreign tradesman, that Harold's arrogant opinion that the British were some kind of superior race was unshakeable. He would never dream of rubbing shoulders with what he condescendingly considered to be Greek peasantry, even though he was the interloper in their country. Obtuse in the extreme, he remained blind to the fact that the proud villagers considered him to be a loathsome, bumptious boor, inflated with his own delusions of self-importance.

Vangelis had assured Maria that 'the' Harold and Joan would love her to explore every nook and cranny of their home and she should feel free to have a good rummage. Whilst I set out to bore Harold rigid, Maria disappeared for a good poke about, sticking her still soot-stained fingers into every foreign curiosity and cackling with derision at the ghastly purple wall-to-wall shag-pile. I felt a tad guilty abandoning Marigold to the company of Joan, but she had entered into the spirit of the mission by taking along a gift of a bottle of toilet bleach she planned to suggest Joan could use to touch up her roots. Harold's face soon matched the shag-pile when he caught Maria testing out the carpet's flammability; in spite of her promise to stop burning plastic Maria clearly found it hard to suppress her pyromaniac tendencies.

Taking advantage of Harold's complete ignorance of any word of the Greek language beyond *beera*, I took it upon myself to pretend to translate Maria's indecipherable comments. When she muttered something in completely inexplicable Greek in response to my stock phrase

that 'my wife is a vegetarian who plays the piano well,' I informed Harold that Maria thought
his shag-pile showed he had execrable taste. I
revelled in putting words into Maria's mouth,
saying the large bathtub they boasted held the
two of them reminded her of the old troughs
they used to bath the pigs in. "She asks if you
got it out of the tip?" I said.

When we stepped out onto the patio Maria
could hardly hold herself back, overcome with
excitement at the sight of the pool. After tentatively lowering her wrinkled body into the water, she splashed around in obvious delight, expressing her sheer joy in indecipherable Greek
which I mistranslated for Harold's benefit as an
enquiry if it was okay that she'd just inadvertently relived herself in his pool. Whilst Joan reacted by screeching in disgust and pouring the
contents of Marigold's gift into the pool, I took
advantage of Harold's open-mouthed horror by
launching into a ponderously dull lecture about
his irresponsible usage of water in a village with
shortages, peppering my boring monologue
with an endless list of tedious statistics.

Strolling home arm in arm a couple of hours

ater, Marigold and I ran into Spiros.

"Victor, I am delighted to see you are looking the old self again after whatever was trou-
bling you. Tell to me, what puts the big smile on
the face?" Spiros asked.

"Oh, I think I can safely say that I skilfully
manipulated Harold into never again inviting
us to one of his ghastly pool parties," I replied.

"Ah yes, Vangelis tell to me you take the
plunge," Spiros said with a knowing wink, having obviously been appraised of my plan by the
builder.

"Victor was quite marvellous, he elevated
the art of being boring to a whole new level,"
Marigold boasted. "Harold was absolutely desperate to get rid of us. He will never invite us
again."

"I'd go as far as to say that he will almost
certainly even snub us in future," I gloated

"Bravo Victor, that is quite the accomplish-
ment," Spiros praised, slapping my back
soundly before going on his way. Doing an
about turn Spiros suddenly called out, "But Victor, what have you done with Kyria Maria?
Vangelis tell me she go with you."

"Maria. Oh she's still splashing round in

Harold's pool. I doubt he'll ever be able to ge
her out of there."

A Note from Victor

All Amazon reviews most welcome.
Please feel free to drop a line if you would like information on the release date of future volumes in the Bucket series.

vdbucket@gmail.com

Printed in Great Britain
by Amazon